Finding Out Ab

FIGHTING IN WORLD WAR II

Sarah Harris

Batsford Academic and Educational Ltd *London*

Contents

The top picture on the front cover is Dwight Shepler's "Battle for Fox Green Beach, Normandy", D-Day (Peter Newark's Western Americana); the left-hand bottom picture shows a 79th Armoured Division Churchill Tank, Normandy, 8 June 1944 (Imperial War Museum); the right-hand bottom picture is part of a leaflet dropped to Prisoners of War in Japan (see page 39).

First published 1983

Typeset by Tek-Art Ltd, London SE20
and printed in Great Britain by
R.J. Acford Ltd
Chichester, Sussex
for the publishers
Batsford Academic and Educational Ltd,
an imprint of B.T. Batsford Ltd,
4 Fitzhardinge Street
London W1H 0AH

ISBN 0 7134 3658 1

ACKNOWLEDGMENTS

The Author would like to thank the following fo their help in the preparation of this book: Pau Bush, Hilda and Ike Davies, Peter Davies Vivienne Griffiths, Elizabeth, Brian and Nic Harris, Walter Hayward, Erica and Max Holley G.F. Osborne, John Tyndall and the Taylor family

The Author and Publishers thank the followin for their permission to reproduce th illustrations: Aurora Publications, Leningra page 41 (bottom); Fleet Photographic Unit, HMS *Excellent* (Crown Copyright), page 15; Geoffre Foster, page 27 (from *36th Division, Th Campaign in North Burma*); The Controller o H.M.S.O., pages 28, 33 (from *The Burm Campaign*, 1946); Imperial War Museum frontispiece and pages 7, 8, 17, 19, 20 (bottom 35, 37; Imperial War Museum Archives, pages 23 40. Other photographs are from private collec tions. Rudolph Britto drew the diagram an maps: page 11 (from *Tanks Across the Desert* ec George Forty), page 26 (from *Phoenix*) and pag 47.

Thanks are also due for permission to us extracts from written sources:
Page 8 "The Battle" from Simpson, *Air wit Armed Men*, London Magazine Editions, 1972
Page 9 "I stood watching" from S. Berlin, *I ar Lazarus*, Galley Press, 1961

continued on page 4

Introduction

The Second World War is an event in history about which most of us think we know a great deal. Films, books, television series, comics – even our language, with phrases such as "Dunkirk Spirit" and "D-Day" – bring it constantly to our attention. The war, or at least Britain's part in the European war against Nazi Germany, has become part of our cultural inheritance, of our race memory.

This makes the historian's job a great deal more difficult. To find out about fighting in the Second World War means separating fact from fantasy; cutting through the layers of national pride and questioning generalization. It means looking at the detail of war; at the men and women who fought it; planned it; survived it; died in it; at its organization; its innovations; its costs and its benefits.

This book looks at some of the aspects of fighting in the war. It uses primary sources, contemporary material and the recollections of men and women who lived through those years. It is not a complete picture; but perhaps the material here will encourage you to look for the detail when you are finding out about fighting in the Second World War.

We date the war from the day when Britain and France declared war on Germany: 3 September 1939. It ended on 14 August 1945.

Britain and France declared war on Germany as a result of Germany's invasion of Poland on 1 September 1939. Since March 1936, German troops had occupied the Rhineland, Austria and Czechoslovakia. For the British public, Poland was the last straw, and the British Government was by now convinced that it had to try to stop Germany's expansion. Britain had always disliked any single country on mainland Europe becoming too strong, and had fought France under Napoleon in the nineteenth century and Imperial Germany in 1914 largely for this reason. Once Britain had made up her mind to fight, France was also willing to go to war.

There was little Britain or France could do to help Poland hold out against the German attack. Their strategy was to weaken Germany's economy by blockading her ports and bombing her factories, while building up their own armed forces for an attack.

Germany did not allow Britain and France time to do this. In April 1940 Norway was occupied and on 10 May 1940 Holland, Belgium and Luxembourg were invaded by the German Army on its way to France. By 22 June all these countries had surrendered, the remnants of the British Army had been rescued from Dunkirk, and Italy had entered the war in support of Germany.

Hitler, the German Führer (leader), hoped that Britain would now withdraw. It had not been part of his plan to defeat her. When it became clear that Britain would not come to terms, an invasion was planned. The German air force, however, failed to gain control of the air – thought necessary for an invasion by sea to succeed. The invasion plans were shelved.

During the spring of 1941, Germany took control of the whole of South East Europe and part of North Africa, where the Italian Army had not been very successful. Then, on 22 June 1941 the Soviet Union was invaded. By the end of November the German Army was in the suburbs of Moscow.

In December 1941 two events changed the course of the war. Firstly, the Soviet Army counter-attacked the Germans and forced them to retreat from the outskirts of Moscow. This, and the paralysing effect of the Russian winter, turned the war in Europe from a series of swift engagements into a long, slow war – much harder for the German economy to pay for.

Secondly, in the Far East, Japan attacked the United States Pacific fleet at Pearl Harbour on 7 December. The Japanese Government was seeking to control much of South East Asia. Japan had already invaded large areas of China. The United States, in an effort to stop Japan dominating the Pacific, had introduced a ban on important exports to Japan, such as oil. Encouraged by Germany's success, Japan decided to attack the American fleet and clear the way for an invasion of Malaya (part of the British Empire) and the Phillipines, which followed on 8 December. Germany was Japan's ally and Hitler declared war on the United States in her support. The entry of the United States into the war meant that, in the end, Germany must be defeated. The economic wealth of the United States would ensure that, given the will to win, she could defeat any country in the world.

It did not seem likely at first. During the first months of 1942 the Japanese Army, Navy and Air Force succeeded in driving south through the Phillipines and Dutch East Indies and west to the frontiers of India. In Europe, the German Army was holding its own. But, at the end of 1942, three victories for the Allies marked the military turning-point of the war. In November 1942 the German and Italian Armies in North Africa were defeated by the British and forced to retreat. In January 1943 the German Army at Stalingrad surrendered to the Soviets, and in that same month the Japanese withdrew from the Pacific Island of Guadalcanal, after the Americans had won a series of engagements.

Through 1943 and 1944 the Germans and Japanese were pressed back, in the Soviet Union, Italy, Burma, the Phillipines, and France. The Allies were only prepared to end the fighting when Germany and Japan surrendered unconditionally — no terms for surrender could be discussed. So it was not until 7 May 1945, after Hitler had committed suicide and the British, Soviet and American Armies met in the middle of Germany, that the German Armed Forces surrendered. In Japan, it was not until over 100,000 citizens of Hiroshima and Nagasaki were killed by two atomic bombs that the Imperial Government surrendered, on 14 August 1945. The fighting was over.

Useful Sources

1. PEOPLE

People you, your parents and your grand-parents know, who served in the Second World War, will be your best source of original information. From them you may be able to collect a wealth of material. If you don't know anyone, your local British Legion branch or branches of the Royal Naval or Royal Air Force Association may be able to help.

a) *Recollections* Talk to Second World War veterans, or rather let them talk to you. Use a tape recorder; don't interrupt; sit patiently through the boring bits — they may trigger off a really interesting memory. Don't worry about the order of events; you can sort that out later; and don't ask too many questions, just to prompt or clarify. Finally, don't be disappointed if it all sounds dull. For most service men and women life was very dull. Even those who were in combat may well find it difficult to talk about; it may have been too horrible; they may still have very angry feelings about it; or quite simply (and this is very common) they just can't remember. Don't press too hard.

b) *Documents* Ex-servicemen and women may well still have their pay-books and discharge papers. You may be lucky enough to know someone who is a hoarder and then you will be able to look at all sorts of treasures: postcards, airgraphs, propaganda leaflets, ships' newspapers, etc.

c) *Diaries* Even the most briefly kept diary can be fascinating. For example, "took Hill 60 today" might refer to a major engagement on which the outcome of a whole battle rested. It is a good idea to read diaries in conjunction with a published history, so that you can pick up this sort of detail.

2. NEWSPAPERS

Your local library may well have copies of the

local newspaper for 1939-45. Local newspapers are a good source for "personal interest" stories.

National newspapers may be on microfilm in the Reference Library, for coverage of the main events of the war.

But remember: most of the time, everyone was determinedly optimistic, and what the press could report was carefully controlled – so be critical in your reading.

3. PUBLISHED BOOKS

There are hundreds of books about the war written by the soldiers, sailors and air-men who served in it. Many of these are very good (as well as enjoyable to read), but again, remember that they present a unique view of the war – for instance, the vast majority were written by officers – and need to be balanced with other, less dramatically presented material.

4. MUSEUMS

a) The Imperial War Museum in London is an excellent source for technical information on the war and puts on specialist exhibitions from time to time, covering the war in more personal detail. The Museum shows documentary films (e.g. *The World At War*) and publishes reproductions of posters and postcards of ships, aircraft, etc.

b) There are specialist service museums you can visit: e.g. the Royal Air Force Museum at Hendon; and many barracks towns have regimental museums, such as that of the South Wales Borderers at Brecon.

Nearly all the material in this book was collected in these ways, to give you a good idea of the variety of material *you* can obtain without too much difficulty. It means, of course, that the book is almost wholly an account of the experiences of British men and women in the war, and though they will have had many experiences in common with men and women of other nationalities engaged in the war, this would be a quite different book if it were about Italian or Soviet or American men and women. If you have relations or penfriends in other parts of the world, you might be able to obtain information about life in other armed services, which would make an interesting comparison with the evidence you can obtain at home.

SOME LESS FAMILIAR SOURCES

Here is some background information on some of the less familiar sources quoted in the book.

The Campaign in Burma H.M.S.O. 1946

This is the official account of the Burma Campaign written by Lieut-Colonel Frank Owen for the Central Office of Information at the request of the South East Asia Command.

Phoenix

This was the official weekly picture paper produced by SEAC for its troops both American and British. Published in Calcutta it was delivered, by air if necessary, to all troops fighting under SEAC Command. It was written and edited by serving soldiers with journalistic experience and first published in February 1945. Many other commands had similar magazines.

The Picture Post

This was a very popular British weekly picture magazine, published by Edward Hulton. The wartime editions contain reports from the fronts as well as recipes and fashion advice.

The Prisoner of War

This was a newspaper published by the Red Cross for Prisoners of War and their families. It contained uncontroversial information and news from the camps.

Service Guides Hello Chaps! This is Bombay

One of several official service guides prepared for men and women being sent overseas. These guide books were intended to help them adjust to the new country and its culture, and reduce the risk of conflict with the local population, by describing customs and taboos.

The Straits Times

This was Singapore's daily newspaper for English-speaking residents. It was not published during the Japanese occupation.

Joining Up

During peace-time, Britain maintained small, professional armed services, but the First World War had proved that a great deal more man-power was needed to fight a modern war. In April 1939 the British Government announced its intention to introduce compulsory military service, but it was not until 2 September that all men between the ages of 18 and 41 were expected to register and were considered liable for call-up. In March 1941 women were required to register too, and in December 1941 an Act of Parliament conscripted women into the armed services and war-essential jobs.

INTO UNIFORM

A WAAF volunteer was asked by the author to write all she could remember in 1983 about her service life forty years ago. Her detailed recollections of initial training give a good idea of what an impact the transition into service life made on her:

I registered with my age group (25) in September 1941. I was deferred as a wife living with a serving officer but wasn't exempt as I had no family. I heard no more about call-up so in October 1942 decided to volunteer. About a month afterwards I was told to report to Kingsway and there met with a group of women. We were to stay together through Initial Training (about a month). We travelled to Illingworth (I think) in Gloucester that same day and made our acquaintance with a Nissen Hut, twenty iron bedsteads, service blankets and sheets and *Biscuits*. 'Biscuits' was the term used to describe the three rectangular straw filled objects which, when placed on a bedstead, became the mattress. The few personal possessions were then left by a locker, misnamed as it had no lock — and we were lined up and taken to the mess for a meal; knife, fork, spoon and enamel mug having been issued. The sequence of events after this is not quite clear. We were paraded, told to strip to pants and bras and moved forward like sheep waiting to be dipped to suffer what to many was the indignity of being declared F.F.I. (free from infection) . . . . The realisation that privacy had been abandoned for the duration dawned on most of us.

The next morning we faced the cold cement floors of the ablutions — basic indeed with no place to put a towel and before all the women using them had finished the floors were awash. We were then Paraded for breakfast. It was after this meal I discovered that one was expected to dip the knife, fork, spoon and mug in a dustbin like container full to the brim with the water of the grey, green, greasy Limpopo River. We had been given a small linen bag with our cutlery and we were expected to place our now 'washed' cutlery into it.

The day was filled by kitting out. Three bras, three very long vests, three grey Celanese Directoire knickers and three pairs of grey lisle stockings plus two pairs of Black Oxford shoes. Three very stiff cotton blue shirts and two uniform jackets, one WAAF cap and cap badge, a great coat and a pair of gloves . . . . We then packed up all our civilian clothes in brown paper and posted them home . . . .

nlisted men in the Argyll & utherland Highlanders at ayonet practice. What points f interest can you gather rom this photograph?

Then came the day we were told we were to be moved: Parade at 6.30 am and transported to the Railway Station without being told our destination. The start of the journey was in darkness, it was November — with blackout and dim blue lamps in the carriage. Name plates in stations had been removed earlier in the war and those on signal boxes so even the coming of daylight yielded no clues as to our whereabouts. It was very disturbing and I was in a friendly country, in the WAAF for which I had volunteered. It made me realise a little of what the Jews must have felt.

But we ended up in Morecambe, where we drilled endlessly on the Promenade and were lectured at in all the public buildings. The lectures fascinated me, mostly delivered by N.C.O.s who recited Parrot Fashion. If they went wrong they promptly said 'As you were' and proceeded to correct their mistake and carry on. The drilling sessions were long and exhausting but they certainly prevented thought — one became an automaton responding everlastingly to commands such as 'Dress to the Right'. We were continually counting — Salute up two three — down two three — break ranks one two three . . .
(A.C.W. Hilda Davies 2133502)

The only unique thing about a member of the armed services was his or her number; this was a successful way of undermining any sense of self — an important part of military training.

The hut; medical parade; washing up; ablutions; posting home civilian clothes; train journey; lectures; drill — Put these experiences in order of importance for convincing the new WAAF intake that they were now service women and no longer civilians. Explain your first and last choices.

The British Army – The Infantry

"The poor bloody infantry" had the hardest job to do, though they were regarded as the lowest level in the military hierarchy – tank-men were thought more dashing, engineers more skilled. But it was the infantry who won the battles, confronting the enemy face to face in the jungles of the Pacific and Asia, in the wadis of the desert, in the villages of Italy and the forests of Central Europe. They were few in number. In an infantry division of 17,000 men, only 4,000 actually carried a rifle and bayonet: less than a quarter. It is popular to assume that the Second World War was a "safe" war for a soldier. For the infantry man it was as dangerous as World War One.

During the First World War, the vast majority of serving soldiers were line officers and riflemen. If the casualty figures for the Second World War are adjusted to allow for the many soldiers whose role it was to support the army, rather than to fight the enemy, the average casualty rates for the army work out at approximately 13% killed and 32% wounded, figures very close to those for the First World War (13.4% and 36.4% respectively). The infantry accounted for three quarters of the battle casualties.

When we read what the men who fought the battles wrote about their experiences, we can gain some insight into the reality of war.

THE BATTLE

Helmet and rifle, pack and overcoat
Marched through a forest. Somewhere up ahead
Guns thudded. Like the circle of a throat
The night on every side was turning red.

They halted and they dug. They sank like moles
Into the clammy earth between the trees.
And soon the sentries, standing in their holes,
Felt the first snow. Their feet began to freeze.

At dawn the first shell landed with a crack.
Then shells and bullets swept the icy woods.
This lasted many days. The snow was black.
The corpses stiffened in their scarlet hoods.

Most clearly of that battle I remember
The tiredness in eyes, how hands looked thin
Around a cigarette, and the bright ember
Would pulse with all the life there was within.

(Private First Class Louis Simpson, 101st US Airborne Division, Germany, 1945)

UNDER ARTILLERY FIRE

We hit the earth with one thud where we had stood. I could feel the exact spot in the small of my defenceless back (I wish to God we had packs on, I thought, I wish to God we had packs on not because they're any *use* but it feels better) where the pointed nose of the shell would pierce skin and gristle and bone and explode the charge that would make me feel as if I had a splitting headache all over for a fiftieth of a second before I was spread minutely over the earth and hung up in trees.
(Stephen Bagnall, 5th East Lancs. Regiment, Caen, France, June 1944)

TIME OUT OF THE LINE

An observer regarding our tousled forms in thick army socks, battle-dress trousers and woollen jerseys, gazing upon our shaven faces, would not perhaps have considered our beds — two blankets spread on a tiled floor, a haversack or a bundle of dirty underwear for our pillows the ultimate in luxury. But he would not know. Everything is comparative. To sleep in this pleasant unrest, to be dry, to be warm, to own a share in a fire, to be freed from duties, to have a roof, to be away from filth and death and wretched tiredness — that is luxury. This is an infantryman's larger portion of heaven.
(Guthrie Wilson, on the Italian Front, 1943)

If you had been an infantryman in the Second World War, what would have kept you going through the "filth and death and wretched tiredness"?

Are there any impressions and experiences that you think all these different accounts have in common? In what ways do they help you build up a picture of an infantryman's war?

The 6th Royal Scots Fusiliers advance across a field in France, 26 June 1944. The smokescreen has been laid to give some cover.

I stood watching the infantry. Without any show of emotion they got up, picked up their PIAT mortars, their rifles and ammunition and walked slowly up the road towards the enemy, with the same bored indifference of a man who goes to a work he does not love . . . . No hesitation, no rush on the part of anybody.
(S. Berlin, 53rd Heavy Field Artillery, France, 1944)

DIGGING IN

At night the infantryman gets some boards, or tin, or an old door and puts it over one end of his slit trench; then he shovels on top of it as much dirt as he can scrape up nearby. He sleeps with his head under this, not to keep out the rain but to protect his head from airbursts . . . . A trench is dug just wide enough for the shoulders, as long as the body and as deep as there is time. It may be occupied for two hours or two weeks. The next time you are near some muddy fields after a rain take a look in a ditch. That is where your man lives.
(Captain Atholl Stewart, Canadian Infantry, Holland, 1944)

The British Army – The Tank Men

The tank, a British invention, had first been used during the First World War at the Battle of Cambrai (20 November 1917). By 1939 the Germans had far overtaken the British in both the numbers and technical sophistication of their tanks and the Panzer Divisions of the German Army swept all before them in the early years of the war. It wasn't until the United States entered the war that the Allies were able to produce tanks in sufficient quantities to challenge the Germans, and even then the Germans retained technical superiority till the end of the war.

TANKS IN THE DESERT WAR

Large numbers of new American tanks were delivered to the Eighth Army in North Africa. Here tank battles could have some of the speed and dash their commanders had imagined for them.

It was late when we got to bed and as the custom was, we formed up in a square, guns facing outwards, with the petrol and ammo lorries inside — just like the old covered wagon days. We adopted this formation every night and the lads used to be able to drive into it in pitch darkness and half asleep. We were up before light and the order came over the air to break out a little and have breakfast — we finally got it about three that afternoon. We had just got on the move and a lot of shelling started and the reports started to come in about tanks. As soon as the fun began, we fanned right out to see what was happening. On the wireless there were ten tanks here, ten there, then someone would report another twenty five. I was sitting in the seat hoping that they were all reporting the same ones. But no, it is an established fact that we took on the 21st Panzer Division that morning and why not, it was 20th November — Cambrai Day! . . . The great thing about this scrap was the fact that we had fought back the crack German division and they had bigger guns and thicker tanks.
(Jake Wardrop, tank driver, 5RTR, on the Crusader Offensive, November 1941)

TANKS IN ITALY

Dashing tank charges were completely out of place in other theatres of the war, where the role of the tank was to give close support to the infantry and consolidate their hard-won positions. By 1943 Jake Wardrop had become a Tank Commander, 5RTR, and he was in Italy. His diary records:

On 21st October we moved at 4.30 to Capua across the bridge . . . . It was an operation this time, we had to capture two villages, Sparanise and Francolise. As we moved up the road, the stuff thinned out until we reached the artillery positions. Past them for about a mile then we pulled off the road. Ahead of us was the infantry line, the 56th, and about four we had orders to move out and back some up for the night. So a troop set off . . . . The road was being shelled and if you ever want a queer sensation, try standing in a tank with your head out of the top going along a road which is being shelled about a quarter of a mile ahead. We were going slowly and making no dust and I didn't think we could be seen, so it was better to just trickle along. In any case, it's always a toss-up, an extra long one might get you, so we carried on nearer and nearer. My heart was doing about a hundred and fifty a minute and just to pass the time I spoke down to the driver, sweet nothing like, "You're doing fine", "Keep her going steady" and such tripe. We made it, one landed just ahead and about ten yards later another just behind. I asked the driver later if my voice sounded queer and he said he didn't hear a thing, the mike had gone dead — they do that sometimes.
(Jake Wardrop, Tank Commander, 5RTR, Italian Campaign)

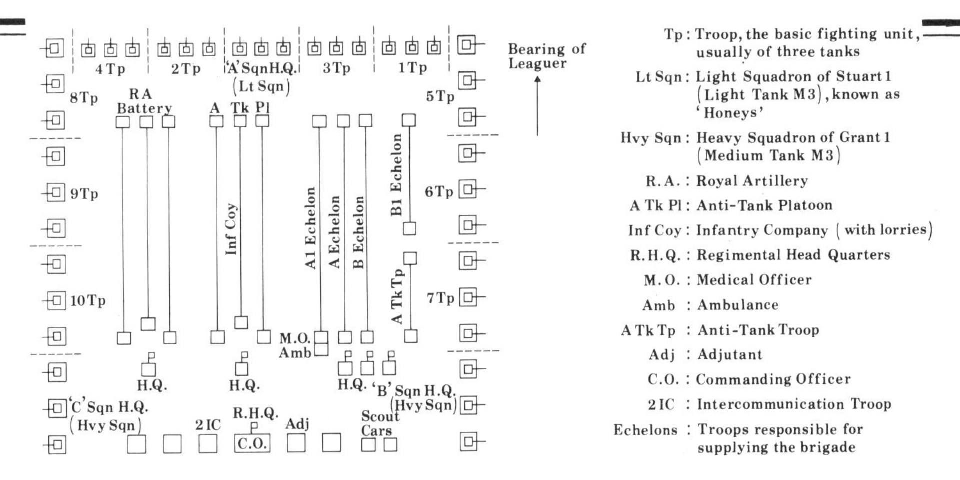

The Box or Protection Leaguer, from 5RTR Battle Drill, November 1942. (This is the "square" referred to by Jake Wardrop — the standard night formation for tanks.) What was the point of this sort of formation?

LIFE IN A CHURCHILL TANK, NORMANDY CAMPAIGN

The regimental history of the Scots Guards contains a description of life in a Churchill Tank:

> **Five men in close proximity, three in the turret and two below in the driving compartment, all in a thick metal oven, soon produced a foul smell . . . . Noise: the perpetual 'mush' through the earphones twenty-four hours each day, and through it the machinery noises, the engine as a background, with the whine of the turret trainer and the thud and rattle of the guns an accompaniment. The surge of power as the tank rose up to the crest of a bank; the pause at the top while the driver, covered with sweat and dust and unable to see, tried to balance his forty tons before the bone-jarring crash into the field beyond.**

There is a photograph of a Churchill Tank on the front cover of this book.

DEATH IN A TANK

Stephen Bagnall, an infantryman serving in Normandy, didn't like tanks but had great admiration for tankmen. Despite his own sense of vulnerability under artillery fire (see page 9), he preferred being out in the open:

> **I would rather have been an infantryman than a tankman any day of the week. It might feel safer inside so long as nothing happens, but you couldn't hope for a pleasant death if anything did happen, shut up in a blazing steel room that was rapidly becoming white-hot and filled with an infernal symphony of fireworks as your own ammunition caught fire and added to the horror . . . . There were escape hatches: and they often stuck. Little blackened dolls about two feet high have been found in tanks. Once they were men.**
> **(Stephen Bagnall, 5th East Lancs. Regiment)**

Would you have felt safer as a Tank Commander with your head sticking out of the turret or as a driver, often unable to see where you were going or what was happening?

The Royal Navy

After the fall of France, in June 1940, Britain became a fortress to which not only arms but also food had to be brought by sea. To a large extent, Britain's ability to stand alone was to depend on the Merchant Navy, whose job it was to bring the goods to Britain, and the Royal Navy, whose job it was to protect the merchant ships from air and sea attack; particularly from the powerful threat of the German "U" Boats (submarines). The Royal Navy was the oldest of the three armed services and a certain kudos was attached to serving in it.

JOINING THE NAVY

I joined up as an Ordinary Seaman at Skegness on New Year's Day 1940. I was 19. I came out on February 26 1946; so I did six years and two months. At Skegness — we were there for about six weeks — they trained people in discipline and routine. I was a chauffeur-gardener before I joined up. Others were bakers, errand boys. I lived in the country. I had never seen a ship. We were green — all green.

My father was in the navy in the First World War — it runs in the family. When I went for my interview I was adamant I was going in the navy . . .

Everyone was trained very, very quickly in the war. They had to get the men to sea. The complement of a destroyer in peacetime might be 80-90, but it rose to 280 in the war. We were tight. I remember I was paid two shillings a day.
(Peter Davies, P/JX 176190, interviewed by the author)

DAILY RATES OF PAY

Promotions, Reductions, Appointments and Alterations in Allotment
(From the Royal Navy Pay Book of C.S. Polson)

RATES OF DAILY PAY	Deduct Allotment Weekly	Net rate to be issued weekly: Figures	Net rate to be issued weekly: Words	Date from which net rate of pay is issuable	Reason for changes in Net Rate (eg Promotions Reductions, Alterations in Allotments etc.)	Officer's Signature Station & Date
3/- +K.V.A.	11/-	13/6	Thirteen shillings & sixpence			4th Sept 1941 HMS Arthur
4/- +K.V.A.	14/-	17/-	Seventeen shillings		Confirmation & declaring allotment	21 Jan 1942 HMS President
5/7 +K.V.A.	25/-	14/-	Fourteen shillings	4th June 1942	Rated LSA & declaration of allotment	1st Sept 1942 HMS Jamaica
Sy.P.O.Ty 6/9 WB 1/0 +K.V.A.	35/-	27/-	Twenty Seven Shillings		Rated Sy.P.O.Ty 24.6.43 Increased allotment to 35/- from 9.9.43	31.8.43 HMS Lucifer
11/- M.A.7/-	Nil	Monthly £27	Twenty Seven Pounds	24 Nov. 1943	Promotion to T.A. Pay Sub.Lieut.RNVR	24/11/43 HMS King Alfred

Allotment: an amount payable directly to dependants through the Post Office
K.V.A.: Kit and Victualling Allowance
L.S.A.: Leading Supply Assistant
M.A.: Marriage Allowance
R.N.V.R.: Royal Naval Volunteer Reserve
Sy.P.O.Ty: Supply Petty Officer Temporary
T.A.Pay: Temporary Acting Paymaster

CONVOY DUTY IN THE NORTH ATLANTIC

G.F. Osborne was in the Royal Navy during the war and served on HMS *Walker*, during the Battle of the Atlantic (1941-42) engaged on escort duty for convoys. He wrote an account of his experiences for the author:

At the beginning of the war I was the engineer officer of an old First World War destroyer, HMS Walker, and I stayed with her until June 1943 . . . .

[After June 1940] we were sent to Liverpool and ran from there in an escort flotilla. We would pick up a convoy outside Liverpool, and sometimes more ships coming down from the Clyde, take them out into the Atlantic for 600 or 700 miles, re-fuel in Londonderry, then pick up a convoy coming in and escort it into Liverpool. This would take about three weeks in all; then we would have three or four days in the Gladstone Dock. There were always some repairs to be done, leaks from fuel tanks and so on. There would be 50 or 60 merchant ships in a convoy, with four or five escorts — two destroyers, two or three frigates. It was pretty deadly dull at sea, terrible weather almost all the time. It was a job to get along the upper deck to the bridge. There were some air attacks on us in the Atlantic but they didn't happen very often. German aircraft (Focke-Wulfs) were mainly shadowing, sending reports of our movements back to Germany. On most convoys, however, we did encounter U-boats and then sometimes we would be at action stations several times during the night.

The U-boat war was at its height at this time. Once they'd made contact the U-boats would shadow the convoy and attack, mostly at night, with torpedoes, and we lost a lot of ships in this way. I saw many of them hit, including several tankers; they would go up in a sheet of flame. We did pick up some survivors from tankers but not many. There were quite a number from other merchant ships; most of them would be in the water and we'd throw ropes and haul them in over the side. On one occasion we had the master and some officers and men of the S.S. 'J.B. White' on board and almost all the crew of the German U-boat which had sunk her and which had in turn been sunk by us — her captain was the German 'ace', Otto Kretschmer. There was a little friction at first but before long they all settled down and got on quite well together. I used to play bridge with Kretschmer and the master and first officer of the merchant ship.
(G.F. Osborne, Engineering Officer, HMS *Walker*)

The Bridge of HMS Walker, *on convoy escort duty in the Atlantic, 1942.*

Does the story about the games of bridge surprise you? Why? Why not?

Write a short conversation which might be taking place between the officer and the seaman in the photograph of HMS *Walker.*

The Royal Navy – HMS *Foylebank*

THE ATTACK ON HMS FOYLEBANK

An extract from the official report of the responsible officer to the commander of the Portland Base, following an incident involving enemy aircraft on 4 July 1940:

To Flag Officer, Portland.
HMS Foylebank lying at "A" Apples Buoy . . . .
Para 3
0825
Report was received from her that a number of aircraft had been picked up by "Cuckoo": bearing 150 degrees. Distance 30-40 miles.
0831
FOYLEBANK ordered to assume first degree readiness. Her position up to then having been that of 4x4 inch and one pom-pom manned.
0835
FOYLEBANK reported that aircraft bore 150 degrees: 15 miles.
0836-0839
Reports were received from "FILTON" that friendly fighter aircraft were approaching from the north.
0840
About 20 Junker dive-bombers appeared over Portland flying in 2 columns at 5,000 feet. They broke formation when over harbour. Five flying on to attack the BLACKHEAD gun position without dropping any bombs: while the remainder attacked FOYLEBANK down-sun. From reports it would seem the first hit on FOYLEBANK was made at 0842 and she was repeatedly hit until 0850. When the aircraft withdrew to southward . . . .
Para 5
Foylebank's 4 inch were seen to be in action but ceased to fire, the pom-poms and the 0.5 machine to fire until the ship was abandoned . . . .
Para 7
Of Foylebank's crew of about 300, 144 men and 13 officers are safe. Details of casualties treated in the RN Hospital are not yet known in full, but reports up to the time of writing give 60.

At the outbreak of war the Royal Navy was in great need of extra ships and took over a number of Merchant Navy vessels, which were converted to war-time use. One such vessel was the *Foylebank*, a cargo ship of the Bank Line. On 26 September 1939 she was requisitioned by the Royal Navy and sent to Belfast to be converted to an anti-aircraft ship. *Foylebank* was equipped with four twin 4" guns, two multiple "pom-poms" and four 0.5 machine guns. She was given radar equipment known as "Cuckoo", and submarine detection gear. On 28 May 1940 she was "commissioned" (formally taken into Royal Navy service) and sent to Portland to complete sea trials and crew training. While at Portland, HMS *Foylebank* also acted as an extra defence for the base and convoy shipping anchored there.

THE AWARD OF THE VICTORIA CROSS

Citation on the award of the Victoria Cross to J.F. Mantle, Leading Seaman P/JX 139070 HMS *Foylebank* (awarded posthumously, 3 September 1940):

Leading Seaman Jack Mantle was in charge of the starboard pom-pom when Foylebank was attacked by enemy aircraft on 4th July 1940. Early in the action his left leg was shattered by a bomb but he stood fast at his gun and went on firing with hand gear only for the ship's electric power had failed. Almost at once he was wounded again in many places. Between his bursts of fire he had time to reflect on the grievous injuries of which he was soon to die but his great courage bore him up to the end of the fight when he fell by the gun he had so valiantly served.

HMS Foylebank *on fire after the attack at Portland,* ▷ *4 July 1940.*

EIGHT MINUTES, THE MORNING OF 4 JULY 1940

A member of the *Foylebank's* crew gives a personal account of the incident, in an interview with the author:

. . . Well what happened? We were there [in Portland]; we were very busy and aircraft coming over continually and while we didn't get attacked a lot — it was the convoys they were after — we became a menace. As an ack-ack ship we were firing at them so they decided one day they'd get rid of us. So on the Tuesday at 4 o'clock, 2nd July a plane came over, took some photos and shot off back again. And they came on the Thursday morning and knocked hell out of us. There were 26 Stukas and they attacked us to get rid of us. And they did get rid of us. They came over at twenty to nine and they attacked us for eight minutes and if you count eight minutes sometime and see how long it is it's a hell of a long time. And during that eight minutes they came down and down; they came down in singles and doubles; they went back again and they came down and we shot three of them down. But what did they leave us with? They left us with 176 dead out of 314 and only about between 30 and 40 not injured. So they scored a victory. They certainly got rid of us. So a lot of the lads who'd joined up only 6 months before — or less — were dead . . . .

* * * *

I was trained in gunnery. There were seven of us on the starboard pom-pom. We went to battle but of the seven of us only two of us came out alive and Johnny Millen, who was one of the lads with us lost a leg at the top and I got a bullet wound in the head and shrapnel . . . . I was in a hell of a way — I was bleeding like a pig. Among that ship's company was a V.C. and that was Jack Mantle who was captain of the gun I was on.

I was on that gun and a bomb came down and blasted us off and that's when they got killed. . . .

I went into hospital — I was in a bad shape — but I got a fortnight's survivors' leave. When I went back the doctor looked at me but said I wasn't fit to go to sea. If you dropped a pin I jumped a mile. It was about a year before I went back to sea.

(Peter Davies, survivor, interviewed 15 January 1983. He was 19 in 1940.)

In what different ways do these pieces of evidence help you form a picture of what happened to the *Foylebank?* Have you enough evidence to form a complete and reliable picture?

Imagine you are a German OR a British newspaper reporter. Write an account of the attack on the *Foylebank* for your paper.

The Royal Air Force–Fighter Command

The success of the fighter pilots in defeating the larger Luftwaffe during the Battle of Britain, and thus helping to prevent the planned German invasion of Britain, has become part of our popular history. The superior design of the Spitfire over the Messerschmidt helped ensure this victory, but so also did the courage and élan of the pilots. Many of the fighter "aces" of the Battle of Britain remain popular heroes today.

The Battle of Britain began on 10 July 1940 with the first major attack by German bombers on convoys in the Channel. It continued throughout July and August, with attacks on airfields and aircraft factories. It ended in September, when the German airforce switched its targets to London and the Blitz began. The aims of the Luftwaffe had been to control the English Channel and defeat the RAF. The switch of targets to the bombing of London (which would achieve neither) was a tacit admission of defeat – though it may not have seemed so at the time.

THE LIFE OF A FIGHTER PILOT IN THE BATTLE OF BRITAIN

Geoffrey Page was twenty years old during the Battle of Britain. He was stationed near London, flying Hurricanes. As the Battle reached its height during August 1940 he describes the increasing pressure under which fighter pilots lived:

The intensity of the air fighting gained momentum and the light hearted battles became sordid reality. Less and less time between flights was spent in idle talk. Sleep became the "Be-all" and "End-all" in life. Climbing out of our machines we threw ourselves on the nearest piece of grass and were asleep within seconds of touching the ground. High powered engines could be ground-tested near our sleeping figures without disturbing us, but the smallest tinkle of the field telephone found us staggering bleary-eyed to our feet.

"Scramble — Angels 15 — 60 plus bandits approaching Dover"

"Scramble — Angels 12 — 90 plus off Ramsgate"

"Scramble — scramble — scramble . . . ."

Life became a nightmare, the centre of which was a telephone bell, and the only sure escape was death . . .

Part of a page from the log book of Pilot Officer M.C.B. Boddington.

YEAR 1940 MONTH	DATE	AIRCRAFT Type	No.	PILOT, OR 1ST PILOT	2ND PILOT, PUPIL OR PASSENGER	DUTY (INCLUDING RESULTS AND REMARKS)	SINGLE ENGINE AIRCRAFT DAY Dual (1)	DAY Pilot (2)	NIGHT Dual (3)	NIGHT Pilot (4)
—	—	—	—	—	—	— TOTALS BROUGHT FORWARD	144.25	164 05		
AUGUST	2.	SPITFIRE U.		SELF		SCRAMBLE.		1.10		
"	4.	F.				PATROL BASE		.50		
"	7.	X.				SCRAMBLE		.40		
"	8.	N.				PATROL (2ND CHANNEL 'BLITZ' 60 E/A DOWN)		2.05		
"	"	N.				RETURN TO BASE FROM EXETER.		40		
"	"	MAGISTER.	3858			DUSK LANDINGS		.40		
"	9.	SPITFIRE Y.				SCRAMBLE		.45		
"	10.	MAGISTER.	3858			NIGHT FLYING		"		.25
"	11.	SPITFIRE T.				PATROL (3RD CHANNEL 'BLITZ' 61 E/A DOWN)		.25		
"	11.	MAGISTER.	3858			NIGHT FLYING				35
"	12.	SPITFIRE T.				CONVOY PATROL 1ST CHASE .00. 2K PLYMOUTH UNCONFIRMED		1.15		
"	12.	"	9319			CIRCUITS & BUMPS				.50.
"	13.	"	9319			SCRAMBLE ANGELS 10 TO PT. 7. ('BLITZ' – 19)		1.50		
"	14.	"	3280			FROM ST EVAL TO MIDDLE WALLOP		1.00		
"	14.	"	"			RAID 2ND CHASE 1. JU. 18 COTTEN. ('BLITZ' – 20)		1.30		
"	14.	"	"			"		.45		

Squadron Leader Stanford Tuck, a fighter pilot "ace". What do the swastikas painted on the plane indicate, do you think?

FIRST KILL

Geoffrey Page goes on to describe his feelings on shooting down his first enemy aircraft and how, eventually, all normal reactions to death and destruction were blotted out of his mind:

Perhaps it was on account of the bombed sailors tending their stricken ship, or perhaps it was in remembrance of Minny, and those others whose names were now forming a long list in my memory. Who knows? Whatever the reason, my Hurricane dived unwaveringly into the stream of enemy aircraft and settled solidly behind the selected victim before opening fire . . .

Closing the gap steadily I waited until the range closed to about a hundred yards. Then, like a man yelling at the top of his voice to relieve pent-up feelings, I pressed the firing button and kept it depressed even after the Stuka had become a flaming inferno in front of my eyes . . .

Twenty minutes later, physically and mentally exhausted, I landed and taxied back to the dispersal pen, a different person. I had taken off from the same air-field an innocent, and returned a bloodied fighter pilot, or was it a murderer hiding behind the shield of official approval?. . .

A few weeks later:

Hardly a day was now passing without some striking event taking place. The death of a friend or enemy provided food for a few moments of thought, before the next swirling dog-fight began to distract the cogitating mind from stupid thoughts such as sadness or pity — remorse had long since died. It was the act of living that perhaps became the most exciting form of occupation. Any fool could be killed; that was being proved all the time. No, the art was to cheat the Reaper and merely blunt his Scythe a little. After all, it was only a game and he was bound to win, but it was fun while it lasted. (Geoffrey Page, Fighter Pilot)

Use the information on these pages to write a personal "diary" for a fighter pilot for three weeks in August 1940.

—The Royal Air Force–Bomber Command—

The aeroplane was a major weapon of the Second World War. As an attacking weapon it could be used to carry bombs deep into the enemy's territory to destroy factories, railways, even whole cities. "Strategic bombing", as it was called, was a new weapon of war. The techniques of bombing raids developed from the rather haphazard flights of the early days to the massive saturation raids of the later years of the war, where hundreds of bombers, carrying larger and larger bombs, were led by specialist navigation planes to the target. This approach to war was expensive, losses among bombers were very high, and the extent of the damage inflicted on German war production and morale is debatable.

A page from the log book of Flight Lieutenant O.R. Matheson, bomber pilot. What was the total flying time for F/Lt Matheson during these nine days? How much of that total was operational flying?

AN RAF RAID ON BERLIN AT NIGHT

Wing Commander Guy Gibson, in his book *Enemy Coast Ahead*, describes a major bombing raid on Berlin in the spring of 1943, when he was Commanding Officer of 106 Squadron:

> **Like a fleet of battleships the force sails in. Above are hundreds of fighter flares, lighting up the long lane of bombers like daylight. Now and then Junkers 88's and Me 110's come darting in and out like black moths trying to deliver their attack. The sky is full of tracer bullets, some going up, some going down. . .**
>
> **On all sides bombers are blowing up, as they get direct hits, great slow flashes in the sky, leaving a vast trail of black smoke as they disintegrate earthwards. Someone bales out.**
>
> **One minute to go — bomb doors open.**

Year 1942 Month	Date	Aircraft Type	Aircraft No.	Pilot, or 1st Pilot	2nd Pilot, Pupil or Passenger	Duty (Including Results and Remarks)	Single-Engine Day Dual	Single-Engine Day Pilot	Single-Engine Night Dual	Single-Engine Night Pilot	Multi-Engine Day Dual	Multi-Engine Day 1st Pilot	Multi-Engine Day 2nd Pilot	Multi-Engine Night Dual	Multi-Engine Night 1st Pilot	Multi-Engine Night 2nd Pilot	Passenger	Instrument Cloud Flying Dual	Instrument Cloud Flying Pilot
						Totals Brought Forward	50 35	102 40	1 15		33·45	265 45	35 55	7 15	155 26	88 20	35 15	19 45	101 30
July	23	LANCASTER	R5610 'G'	SELF.	AND CREW.	N.F.T.						·30							
July	23	LANCASTER	R5610 'G'	SELF.	AND CREW.	NIGHT OPERATIONS. Target at DUISBURG.									3·45				
July	25	LANCASTER	R5610 'G'	SELF.	AND CREW.	SCAMPTON - ABINGDON AND RETURN. N.F.T.						1·20							
July	26	LANCASTER	R5610 'G'	SELF.	AND CREW.	N.F.T. AND BEAM APPROACH.						·45							
July	26	LANCASTER	R5610 'G'	SELF.	AND CREW.	NIGHT OPERATIONS. TARGET AT HAMBURG.									5·05				
July	28	LANCASTER	R5610 'G'	SELF.	AND CREW.	N.F.T.						·30							
July	29	LANCASTER	R 5610 'G'	SELF.	AND CREW.	NIGHT OPERATIONS. TARGET AT SAARBRUCKEN.									5·00				
July	31	LANCASTER	E5669. 'E'	SELF.	AND CREW.	NIGHT OPERATIONS. TARGET AT DUSSELDORF									5·05				
Grand Total (Cols. (1) to (10)) 798 Hrs. 15 Mins.						Totals Carried Forward	50·35	102·40	1·15		33·45	265·50	35·55	7·15	174·20	88·20	35·15	19·45	101·30

A Lancaster Avro Mk. 1. The Lancaster carried a crew of seven and was in extensive use by the RAF by the middle of 1942.

The bomb aimer is still counting.
"Fifty seconds."
"Forty seconds."
There is flak all round now. The leading wave of bombers has not been broken up, a few have been shot down, but the rest have held their course. But the short time that they held that course seemed like a lifetime. . .
"Thirty seconds" . . .
"Twenty seconds".
"Steady — hold it" — and then the bomb aimer shouts: "Bombs gone". There is a note of relief in his voice . . .
A volcano is now raging down below, great sticks of incendiaries are still slapping across the point where the target markers had first gone in. . . . Cookies are exploding one after another with their slow red flashes, photo flashes are bursting at all heights as each aircraft takes its photographs. This is a galaxy of light, a living nightmare. . . .
A few leaflets drift down through the bluish glare, only to be burnt in the flames of the burning houses.

From the evidence on these pages, what do you think might have made the life of a member of a bomber crew particularly stressful?

THE STRAIN

In more reflective mood, Guy Gibson wrote:

As we flew above the clouds in those early mornings over the cold North Sea, it seemed to me that the very anvil tops of the cumulus storm clouds were all pointing the way to Germany, as if to say, "That is the way; that is the way to Germany, and you won't come back." Now and then a flash of lightning would make me jump vertically in my seat as at the same time I went into a vertical turn with Mac shouting: "Flak, flak", in the background. I was getting nervy, there was no doubt about it; this bombing was beginning to get me down. . . .

Even when back in bed I could not sleep but used to lie awake at night tossing and turning, thinking of the noise of the engines and that bok-bok noise which was always in my ears. And when I did dream it was always slow motion dreams of balloon cables, thick ones, like tree trunks, which I would get past by landing my aircraft in the middle of Hamburg and cutting them down with an axe, then flying home as if nothing had happened.

Women in the Armed Services

The female sections of the armed services had been established in the First World War. In the Second, where it took the services of 35,000 soldiers to support an infantry division in the front line, their contribution in releasing men for work nearer the front was vital. This meant, however, that the vast majority of women in the services were expected to carry out the most boring, mundane and routine tasks at home. Some, however, manned anti-aircraft guns and ferried aeroplanes (previously the preserve of men), and others, especially the nurses, served close to the front line in difficult and sometimes dangerous positions.

Delivering the clean laundry round Prestatyn Army Camp, 1940. Do you think this was the most efficient way to deliver clean sheets? Can you think of a better one?

The first women to arrive on the Normandy beach-head after "D"-Day were members of Queen Alexandra's Imperial Military Nursing Service. Here they make their beds in a slit trench where they will be protected if bombing occurs. The photograph was taken by an official war photographer for possible publication. What impression is it trying to convey? Do you think it gives an accurate picture? Contrast this slit trench with the description on page 9.

SERVING WITH AN ANTI-AIRCRAFT UNIT

A. Laws was in the ATS from 1942-45. Here are some extracts from her diary for 1944, when she was stationed at Leigh on Sea:

11th October 1944

O misery! The rain beats a loud pit-pat on the tent and the wind blows strong and blustering from the south. The lamp gives out a poor-spirited effort as a light and I have to stand beside to write. There are several new leaky places in the tent and it flaps and bellows so with the wind we have visions of it flying away in the night . . .

We washed the floor boards this afternoon. What a waste of energy . . .

Sheet changing day but the clean sheets aren't in yet.

16th October 1944

Am writing in the nissen hut by the command post. The alarm will go at either 20:15 or 22:15 unless they start a different time table and again in the morning at about 02:15 or 05:00. The Germans like set times, which can be useful . . .

If only it would stop raining. It's black dark and pouring now . . .

Later

The first alarm is over. A doodle with the very first round! And our men on the gun that fired it! We brought down the second little brute too, but after that nothing came within range . . . . We were in a state of excitement . . . eating chips and drinking cocoa and talking ten to the dozen. We shall never sleep tonight. Jessie thinks that the Major was going to kiss her. We shall probably do something awful tomorrow.

SERVING IN THE WAAF, RAF BENSON 1942-44

After her initial training, Hilda Davies was given a job in Administration, primarily because she held a University Degree. She was posted to RAF Benson in Oxfordshire. In her recollections of life in the WAAF, written for the author, she describes her experiences there:

Duty as an A.C.W.Admin. was boring beyond description. I trailed round the camp delivering rolls of toilet paper to Airmen's Married Quarters, now used as WAAF billets. I found that I could, with luck, open the front door and if the bathroom door was open at the top of the stairs toss the toilet roll up and so avoid endless climbing. I began to resent shut bathroom doors. I made tea for WAAF Officers — there were four of them in Admin. whose attitude to Other Ranks was rather that of mistress to servant. I dusted their desks and sat in the outer office waiting to be told what to do next . . . .

I asked for re-mustering and applied for telephonist training. I enjoyed being a telephonist. To work watches rather than a routine day gave me more opportunity to go into Oxford and cycle round the countryside. The work gave me real contact with all ranks and it was a relief to be under the command of RAF Officers. Before D-Day I was posted to Tactical Air Force H.Q. where I was N.C.O. in charge of the exchange. As such I received Eisenhower's message announcing the D-Day landings.

Do the two written accounts suggest any common experiences?

Conscientious Objectors

Once a country decides to conscript men and women (i.e. passes a law which makes service in the armed forces compulsory for those called up), there is the immediate difficulty of what to do with those who refuse to serve; especially if their refusal is based on a deeply held conviction. Conscientious Objectors – those opposed to the war on the grounds of conscience – had been very badly treated during the First World War and, although ill-treatment and public ridicule were far less common during the Second World War, it still required a lot of courage to stand out from the crowd and refuse to bear arms.

600,000 men and women sought exemption from Military Service during the Second World War. Many of them were pacifists and therefore opposed to war of any kind, usually on religious grounds. Some registered political objections to this war in particular – refusing to fight in a war which they saw as being against the interests of working-class men and women. Of these 600,000, 3,500 were granted unconditional exemption; 29,000 were required to work in agriculture; 15,000 were required to do non-combatant duties in the army; and the rest had their cases dismissed. Of these last, 5,000 were prosecuted and the majority sent to prison.

MAKING THE STAND

Edward Blishen was a young reporter when war broke out. He had made up his mind at school that he would not fight and in his book *A Cackhanded War* he remembers what it felt like not to be one of the crowd:

My time for registering came in the spring of 1940. France was falling, and on the morning when I had to go to the Labour Exchange, I'd read of the German units "seeking to make contact" with the fleeing French: and I remember thinking *that* was such a friendly phrase for such a murderous activity: and I remember, too, the shock of knowing that France was finished, and the voice within me saying, "You can't . . . you can't not be in it, now. Not now they've done this to France."

But all that literature of disgust I'd read, bitter fruit of the Great War (as we'd called it till this greater war came) . . . the horror of it, the rejection it expressed, had run in my veins, until I could not think of fighting without a sense of shock. It had been horrible, they had all hated it, those chroniclers of the first world war, and one couldn't, having supped of their anger and revulsion, start it all again. If war began — I'd been very clear about this, in my last year at school, — one would be tempted, the flood would seek to carry one with it; but only by intolerable betrayal of all those haggard men of the first war, I thought . . . could one give in.

So as I made my leaden way to the Labour Exchange, I heard that voice within me, weeping for France, as the voice of disloyal temptation; and I registered as an objector. I was sent to the bottom of the buzzing room, alone, away from the others; and it felt as though I was separating myself from the world . . .

NATIONAL SERVICE (ARMED FORCES) ACT, 1939.
Certificate of Registration in Register of Conscientious Objectors.

D.O. 12 Case No. 2210.

Date 15 FEB 1941

Holder's Name BUNNEWELL. Leonard Frank

Home Address 108 Middlegate Street. Gt Yarmouth

Date of Birth 14. 9. 06.

Holder's Signature

This is to certify that the above person by order of the competent Tribunal is—

*Delete alternative before issue.

*(a) ~~registered unconditionally in the Register of Conscientious Objectors.~~

*(b) registered conditionally in the Register of Conscientious Objectors.

W. Harrison

(Divisional Controller, Ministry of Labour and National Service Eastern Division.)

READ THIS CAREFULLY.

Care should be taken not to lose this certificate, but in the event of loss application for a duplicate should be made to the nearest Office of the Ministry of Labour and National Service.

If you change your home address or your name you must complete the space on the other side of this certificate and post it at once. A new certificate will then be sent to you.

A person who uses or lends this certificate or allows it to be used by any other person with intent to deceive, renders himself liable to heavy penalties.

N.S. 62. *43084 9/39 702

Councillor Bunnewell's C.O. registration card.

RELIGIOUS OBJECTORS

Edward Blishen was required to do agricultural work and was sent, with other objectors, to the East of England to do "ditching, hedging and land clearance". He described some of the other Conscientious Objectors he met on the train journey to their new work:

Oliver was one of the Particular People, and the grounds of his objection to fighting, which he'd explained to me on the train, were so intricate, and rested on such a curious reading of so many unfamiliar parts of the Bible, that I regarded him with something like awe, as one might some eminent cryptogrammatist . . .

Facing us . . . was the Quaker, Billy Grantham. He was, I felt, the most normal-looking of us all . . . . The emotional orderliness which he derived from being a quaker made him, in fact, seem almost conventional: a member of the pacifist establishment. The rest of us were first-generation objectors . . . but Billy was secure in the traditions of his non-conformity.

A POLITICAL OBJECTOR

Leonard Bunnewell was a member of the Independent Labour Party, which opposed the war, believing it to be a capitalist war, fought by the rich and powerful against the interests of the workers. He secured conditional exemption but, as a local councillor, he was subject to public harrasment.

A letter to the local paper:

February 14th 1941
Sir,

With disgust I read in last week's "Mercury" that Councillor L.F. Bunnewell is a C.O. This, I hope, is an exception rather than a rule for Labour . . .

Might I ask if he holds a ration book? If so it is from our brave merchantmen that he is taking food. Does he possess a gas mask? Surely Hitler won't bother to gas him!

Yours faithfully,
"More Proud than Ever to be a Tory"

Could you write a reply to this letter, arguing the case for individual conscience?

Fighting in the Desert

The first major victory of the British in the Second World War was at the Battle of El Alamein, in November 1942. Here the Eighth Army defeated the Afrika Corps and began the long advance which led to the withdrawal of all Axis troops from North Africa by May 1943.

El Alamein was a small railway station near the sea in the Egyptian desert. For two years the war had waged back and forth over this inhospitable landscape. It could be freezing cold at night, boiling hot by day. Sandstorms could blow up at a moment's notice, obscuring all vision. Rainstorms could bog down all transport and tanks in minutes, but there was never enough water. The desert was known as "The Blue" to the men of the Eighth Army.

COPING WITH DESERT LIFE

In the spring of 1942 Jake Wardrop was in the Libyan Desert during a lull in the fighting. He wrote:

> As the summer wore on it got hotter and hotter, we were, as usual, well down in the desert, our spiritual home, and it was thought there wouldn't be a push that summer. We used to get some beer, American tinned, and by buying up tins from the non-drinkers, Stan, George and I had a few mild sessions. At odd times, too, we'd get a bottle of whisky from one of the officers and that would be a big night. During the end of April and the beginning of May there is a hot wind blows up from the Sahara, it is called the *Khamseen* and blows for fifty days and nights — the word is Arabic for fifty. We were camped a few miles to the east of Bir Hakeim and it was very hot indeed. Stanley and I had worked out a theory about the sun, roughly that you had to stay on your feet, if you lay down in the afternoon it had licked you: so we covered ourselves with gun oil and went walking. We used to sit and talk a lot and watch for fires at the other tanks and sidle across and say, "Oh you're making tea". The water was very scarce, so was tea and sugar, but we managed. I sat all day in the sun and made a dun-dial on the ground out of little twigs and small shells. It was accurate for about a week then as the sun was going south to Capricorn it was out and it got worse — I often wondered how the sun-dials in the parks work, perhaps it has something to do with the angle the points make to the face. We used to gaze at the stars a lot and became quite good at telling the time by the plough.
>
> (Jake Wardrop, tank driver, 5RTR)

◁ *British armoured divisions advance towards Tripoli, January 1943.*

EIGHTH ARMY

ersonal Message from the
ARMY COMMANDER

1—When I assumed command of the Eighth Army I said that the mandate s to destroy ROMMEL and his Army, and that it would be done as soon as were ready.

2—We are ready NOW.

The battle which is now about to begin will be one of the decisive tles of history. It will be the turning point of the war. The eyes of the ole world will be on us, watching anxiously which way the battle will swing.

We can give them their answer at once, "It will swing our way."

3—We have first-class equipment; good tanks; good anti-tank guns; plenty artillery and plenty of ammunition; and we are backed up by the finest air king force in the world.

All that is necessary is that each one of us, every officer and man, uld enter this battle with the determination to see it through—to fight and kill—and finally, to win.

If we all do this there can be only one result—together we will hit the emy for "six," right out of North Africa.

4—The sooner we win this battle, which will be the turning point of war, the sooner we shall all get back home to our families.

5—Therefore, let every officer and man enter the battle with a stout heart, d with the determination to do his duty so long as he has breath in his body.

AND LET NO MAN SURRENDER SO LONG AS HE IS NWOUNDED AND CAN FIGHT.

Let us all pray that "the Lord mighty in battle" will give us the ctory.

B. L. MONTGOMERY,
Lieutenant-General, G.O.C.-in-C., Eighth Army.

IDDLE EAST FORCES,
23-10-42.

◁ *General Montgomery's message to his troops at the opening of the Battle of El Alamein.*

If you had been with the Eighth Army, would this message have raised your morale? How would you have felt on reading it? Would it have been more effective broadcast over the radio?

KEEPING UP THE MORALE

On 27 February 1943 the *Picture Post* reported an interview with General Montgomery, the Officer Commanding the successful Eighth Army:

"Morale is the thing," says General Montgomery. "You can do anything with an army when morale is high. Your troops must be in that frame of mind where they want to fight, where they are anxious to meet the enemy in battle." And what is his recipe for securing this high state of morale? In one word — success. But more important than knowing the recipe is being able to apply it.

Even General Montgomery, that Spartan liver and hard trainer, confesses that warfare in the desert is "hard". "The men," he says, "may go without bathing for six months because of the scarcity of water." They feel acutely the loneliness of the desert darkness "under the silent expanse of night far from home and loved ones."

Is there any evidence in the extract from Jake Wardrop that supports General Montgomery's view of the difficulties of desert life?

Fighting in the Jungle

Burma fell to the Japanese in May 1942. The quickest way to recapture it would have been to mount an amphibious assault on Rangoon; but the campaign in Burma was always last on the list for equipment, supplies and armour – the Fourteenth Army referred to themselves as "The Forgotten Army". Without this equipment the only way to win back Burma was by a long and costly operation, launched south from the Indian frontier, fought through dense jungle, in an appalling climate, foot by foot, yard by yard, mile by mile.

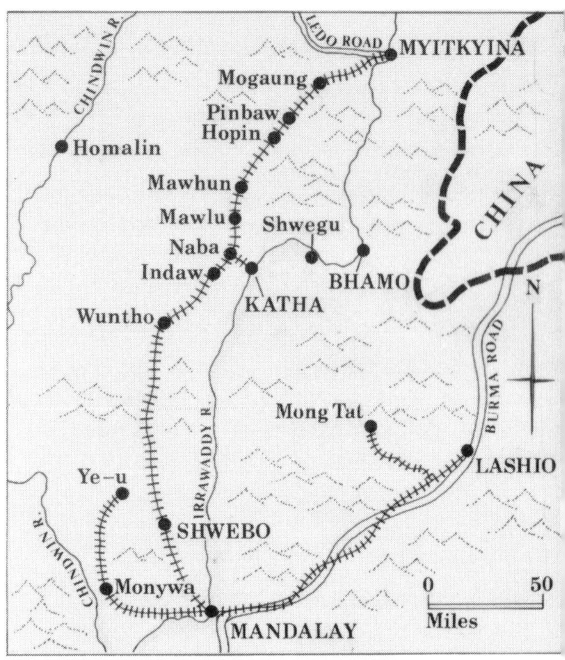

The route from Myitkyina to Mandalay – the key to Central Burma.

JUNGLE WARFARE

Captain George Yates, serving with the 14th Army, wrote an article for his local newspaper (*The Northern Daily Telegraph*) while on leave from Burma. He described some of the immense difficulties of fighting in that country:

It is thickly wooded, with most of the maps marked, "dense, mixed jungle, mainly bamboo." What these words can mean can only be fully appreciated by those who have fought their way through it, who have been ambushed in it by enemy they cannot see, and cannot locate because the hills re-echo the bursts of fire. The hills rise from the plain like rivets on a billiard table, and between them flow the countless chaungs and wide, sluggish rivers. Over all hangs the atmosphere of the jungle, and in it all lie those scourges of the tropics, malaria, cholera, dysentery, black-water, leeches, snakes and other unpleasant inhabitants of an unpleasant part of the world.

Through this, British, Indian, Ghurka and African soldiers are advancing, maintained by long and slender lines of communication which may cross mountain ranges 9,000 feet high by precipitous jungle paths, or be simply represented by a line denoting aircraft supply. They are advancing against an enemy trained to fight in that country and imbued with the spirit of Samurai, which is literally death before dishonour, in fact, an honour to die in battle.

It is an essentially personal war. Seldom is the enemy more than 25 yards away, and as often as not a battle develops into a number of small fights which may involve anything from a section to an individual, savage merciless fighting with no quarter given or asked for.

Men of 36th Division, crossing a chaung in the ▷ Railway Corridor.

ADVANCE DOWN THE RAILWAY CORRIDOR AUGUST-DECEMBER 1944, MYITKYINA TO KATHA

In July 1944 the 36th Division of the 14th Army was given the task of clearing the Japanese from the Railway Corridor in North Burma. A report of their campaign was published in *Phoenix*, the official SEAC magazine, in March 1945:

> The only real way south from Myitkyina to Mandalay is via the single-track railway which runs through Mugaung, Naba . . . Indaw and Shwebo. . . . there are no roads north of Mandalay — only tracks which at their best are barely fit for bullock carts . . .
>
> The valley down which we advanced was, until November, a flat stretch of marshland due to the monsoon, intersected with chaungs (river courses flooded in the rainy season, dry beds at other times) running awkwardly across the route. What was once rich paddy-land along the floor of the valley has been allowed to stagnate under Jap occupation so that it became overgrown with thick elephant grass, often 10 feet high, and treacherous not only because it provided cover for enemy positions, but also because, in the rainy season, it disguised knee-deep bog. With the end of the rains, you get thick dazzling white dust, and then although the temperature gets down to an average of 65 degrees in January, it warms up to 105 again by April before the monsoon starts. (Hedley Shepherd, with 36th Division)

VILLAGES EN ROUTE

Geoffrey Foster was the Chief Doctor, serving with 36th Division, in their advance through Burma. He wrote a personal history of its activities, on the sea voyage home, and published it for private circulation among his comrades:

> Pinbaw had little to commend itself. It was really only a collection of wooden houses on stilts, situated in a sea of mud, slime, filth and smells. . . . Like most other places Mawlu was no holiday resort . . . . But for some reason or other, everyone seemed imbued with the prospect of Katha and a glimpse of the Irrawaddy, though what they expected to find there God alone knows. . . . It could never be described as an inviting sort of place. The river, a conveyor of driftwood and corpses, was dirty, muddy . . . and owing to its filth, was rendered quite unfit for bathing . . . . Indaw had even less to boast about and merits no attempt at description.

Do you think these places were really as Geoffrey Foster described? If you think they were, explain what might have made them so unpleasant; if you don't, what do you think caused Geoffrey Foster to write of them as he did?

Supplying an Army

Not only does a fighting army need the basic equipment for war – tanks, guns, machine-guns, transport – but also it needs the "every-day" things such as food, drink, petrol, ammunition and medical supplies. Without them, not even the most determined soldier can fight on.

SUPPLY DROPS IN BURMA

The problem of supply was most difficult in Burma, where entire divisions had to be supplied by air if the fighting was to continue. During the famous battle of the Admin Box (February 1944), supplies had to be dropped with great accuracy into an area less than a mile square, surrounded entirely by the Japanese.

> **Supply dropping is itself an art. The aircraft must fly at minimum height and speed during the process. . . . To complete an accurate drop it must make at least eight circuits over the dropping zone. During this half-hour the pilot must keep his heavy ship trim, or else the parachute will get tangled in his rudder as the loads tumble out of the doorway. For the crew it means a violent and unceasing effort to haul the crates and sacks the length of the "hold" as far as the open door, poise and push them clear. . . .**
>
> **In Arakan 900 sorties carried 3,000 tons into battle. With food, ammunition and weapon replacements came cigarettes, kit, oil, petrol, the mail, even beer. Tank troops waiting for fuel watched drums of it cascading down on parachutes. Before the aircraft left the armour was moving into action. The twin-engined transport planes were sitting birds for enemy fighters and ground fire. But only one was lost, and she, too, delivered her goods.**
> **(The Burma Campaign, HMSO, 1946)**

FOOD IN THE FRONT LINE

Towards the end of the desert campaign, officials began to recognize that, although the rations for the troops represented an adequate diet, they were so boring that the men often failed to eat them. The new "compo" rations were introduced into Tunisia in late 1942, with the emphasis on variety as much as on food value, and these were the rations issued to front line troops till the end of the war. Lieutenant Peter Royle recalls the contents:

"Compo rations" was a wooden box containing enough food for 14 men for 1 day. We lived on it for the next five months.

1. A tin of tea, sugar, milk in powder form. Boiling water added, gave you a hot sweet liquid which hardly tasted of tea but was a life saver.

2. 14 bars of thick plain chocolate.

3. A large tin of biscuits. The nearest thing to match these today would be a dog biscuit because they were very tasteless and hard. I used to nibble my chocolate and a biscuit at the same time and it was similar to a chocolate biscuit if your imagination was good. The cooks used to make biscuit porridge as a change — just tip a quantity of broken up biscuits into boiling water and when they had softened up, there was your porridge. . . .

4. Tins of stew or meat pudding.

5. Tins of Bully Beef — generally eaten cold . . .

6. Tins of pudding. These were a great favourite of mine and there were three or four varieties. Mixed fruit, marmalade, jam and syrup. There was always a touch of excitement about the puddings as you never knew what flavour it was until you opened the tin after cooking it.

7. Tin of 100 cigarettes which gave every man an average of 7 a day.

8. Tins of sausages or bacon which were heated and then served from the tin. The sausages averaged out at about 2/man/day and were really quite palatable but the bacon was very fatty and was salted with greaseproof paper inside the tin.

9. Sardines. I used to eat mine on a biscuit as the oil soaked into the biscuit and softened it up.

10. Tin of jam — generally plum or apricot . . .

11. There was probably some salt and boiled sweets.

(Lieutenant Peter Royle, Royal Artillery, Tunisia, 1942/3)

You are responsible for supplying a division (17,000 men) with their compo rations for a two-week campaign. How many wooden boxes must you make up? How many sausages is that? Can you make up five different dinner menus from the contents of the box?

A supply drop into the Admin Box in Arakan. Why do you think "inessentials" like mail, cigarettes and beer were dropped?

Contact with Home

During the Second World War some servicemen and women were away from home for almost the whole of the duration. Many others spent a year or more on active service overseas, with no home leaves. Contact with home was thought of as very important in maintaining morale. Members of the armed forces could send mail home at cheap rates, service papers contained news from the home front, parcels could be sent and received and famous stars from home came to entertain the troops in the front line.

A festive air-graph for Christmas 1944. The original message was written on a special form measuring 10″ x 8″ – four times the size of the actual air-graph. The message area on the form was 8″ x 8″. A miniature negative was taken and sent. A photographic print, of which this is an example, was made at the destination and delivered. The batch number (176930) could be used to trace the original if that particular pile of mail was lost in transit, and the message could be re-sent. The same system was used by the troops to send messages home.

What was Max Holley's rank and ship? Can you tell where he was for Christmas 1944? Explain your answer. ▷

VISITING STARS

The SEAC magazine reported:

> **George Formby and Beryl**
> **Highest-paid British film star George Formby brought wife and partner Beryl, comedian Tony Heaton, pianist Gerald Benson, four banjoleles, one uke and a mini-piano here, hoping to lead them all into Mandalay to the tune of his new song "Mr. Wu is in the Air Force Now". . . The Formby's went to Italy on D-Day plus 2, following the Eighth Army from Sicily. They managed to do that by swapping autographs with a brigadier, his signature being on a movement order.**
> **(*Phoenix*, 17 March 1945)**

George Bush added the note "Going into first action", explaining when he sent this postcard, after the war. Why do you think he sent a postcard rather than a letter at such a time? ▽

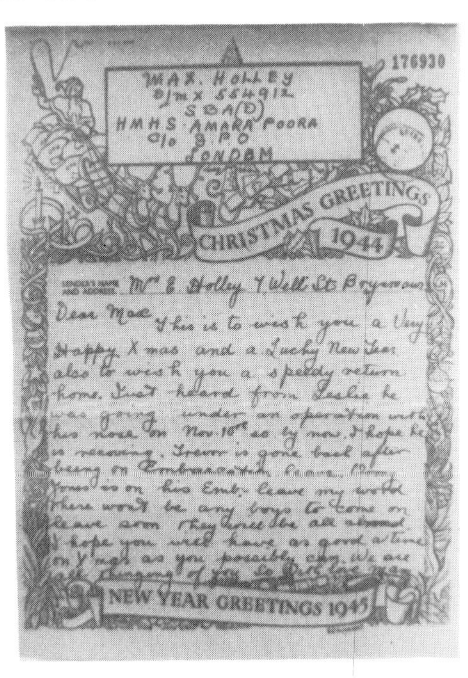

176930

MAX. HOLLEY
D/MX 564912
SBA(D)
HMHS AMARA POORA
C/o G.P.O
LONDON

CHRISTMAS GREETINGS 1944

Mrs E. Holley 7 Well St Brynmawr

Dear Max
This is to wish you a Very Happy X mas and a Lucky New Year also to wish you a speedy return home. Just heard from Leslie he was going under an operation with his nose on Nov. 10th so by now I hope he is recovering. Trevor is gone back after being on Embarkation [illegible] [illegible] is on his Emb. Leave my [illegible] there won't be any boys to come on leave soon they [illegible] all abroad I hope you will have as good a time on X'mas as you possibly can. We are all thinking of you [illegible]

NEW YEAR GREETINGS 1945

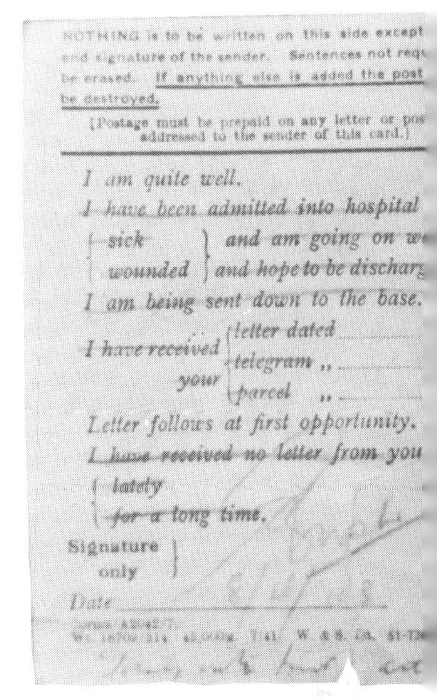

NOTHING is to be written on this side except the date and signature of the sender. Sentences not required may be erased. If anything else is added the post card will be destroyed.

[Postage must be prepaid on any letter or post card addressed to the sender of this card.]

I am quite well.
~~I have been admitted into hospital~~
~~sick~~ } and am going on we[ll]
~~wounded~~ } and hope to be discharg[ed]
~~I am being sent down to the base.~~

~~I have received~~ your { letter dated ……
telegram ,, ……
parcel ,, ……

Letter follows at first opportunity.
~~I have received no letter from you~~
{ ~~lately~~
{ ~~for a long time.~~

Signature only } [illegible]

Date [illegible]

Going into first act[ion]

PARCELS

Information for troops serving in India, from *Hallo Chaps! THIS IS BOMBAY*, a guide for service people, 1943:

"DUTY FREE" PARCELS. All ranks can send *four* "Duty Free" parcels in one year to the U.K. Normal postage rates will be charged.

These parcels *must not* weigh more than 5lb (including packing); exceed 30s. (Rs 20) in value; contain drinkable spirits; contain more than ¼ pint of scent; contain more than ½lb. total weight of tobacco, including cigars and cigarettes (200 cigarettes or 50 cigars = ½lb.) nor tobacco marked "H.M. Ships only"; contain any imported article; contain more than 2lb. of any one foodstuff (tea 1lb); contain any communication other than the name and address of the sender.

A Christmas parcel for a soldier serving in North Africa. It includes books, Marmite, biscuits, pickle and sweets.

Make a list, in order of importance, of the things you would most like to have heard about/had from home if you had been serving overseas for three years.

NEWS FROM THE HOME FRONT

Phoenix included news from London:

The Conservative Party conference, under the chairmanship of the Right Hon. R.A. Butler M.P., has been the most popular offering recently, with Mr. Churchill in the starring role. . . . Speakers were carefully chosen and said what the audience expected them to say without stirring either provocation or dissension . . .

The victorious advance of Allied armour into liberated and conquered territories brings in its wake problems of the peace to come. . . . The most serious of these is the possibility of the meat ration, established since 1941 at 1s 2d per person, dropping below the shilling per head which is regarded by some as a nutritious minimum. The necessity to supply victims of Nazi occupation with food is one of the reasons . . .
One of the most attractive musical events of recent years has just taken place at the Albert Hall. . . . It was a concert in memory of the late Sir Henry Wood, founder and for fifty years conductor of the world-famous Promenade Concerts. (*Phoenix*, 28 April 1945)

Injury and Death

RETURN TO CONSCIOUSNESS

In the summer of 1940, Geoffrey Page's Hurricane caught fire during an air battle and he received terrible burns to his face and hands. He spent two years in hospital and underwent many operations before returning to active flying duties. He describes his return to consciousness after the first of the skin-graft operations on his hands:

Now I had a glimmering of what Christ must have felt as they drove the nails through his hands. The nails were many and they were being hammered inexpertly through the same hand, only to be withdrawn agonisingly with huge pincers. The hammering torture came from a distance, or so it seemed, but it was there nevertheless. Wildly I tossed my head from side to side on the sweat damped pillow. "No. . . . no. . .n. . .n. . ." The moan came as a disbelief that such things could be, were allowed to be. Like a frightened animal being stroked, I calmed down as gentle fingers wiped my wet forehead with gauze.

"Lie still and we'll give you something for the pain."

Fuzzily through the mists of the lingering anaesthetic I heard the words. A shuddering moan escaped my lips as the nails were wrenched out for the tenth time. My head started its wild tattoo. This time Sister Hall made no attempt to sooth her patient, but swiftly set about administering the injection of morphia. The prick of the needle was unfelt in the sea of pain. Soon my head stopped its senseless rolling and torture disappeared over the horizon as the drug began its calming effect . . .

(Geoffrey Page, Fighter Pilot)

During the Second World War there were more deaths in the civilian populations of the countries at war than in their armed services. This was partly a result of the policy of slaughter against Jews, East Europeans and ethnic minorities, adopted by Nazi Germany. It was also a consequence of the use of aerial bombardment against civilian populations, adopted by both the Allies and Germany.

But combat necessarily means risking injury and death, and for those men who fought in the front line, in the air, at sea or on land, the risks were very great; in some cases they had as high as a 75% chance of being killed. For the whole British army serving overseas, including all administrators, suppliers and others not directly involved in the fighting, nearly 22% became battle casualties and one in three of these were deaths.

FIRST ENGAGEMENT

Round a bend in the hedge a man was kneeling down. His head was touching the ground so that he might have been making an obeisance before some Eastern Ruler. John Gregory was bending over him, a hand on his shoulder. As I drew near John stood up and said:

"I'm afraid he's had it."

I thought how surprising for I could see no mark.

"Who is it?"

"Holden."

We had two Holden's in our company and I assumed it was the one I knew least well. Here I will have to say something that will sound callous but is not intended to be callous. I had known that people would be killed and I had resigned myself to losing those whom I did not like or whom

The caption to this picture in the official history of ▷ The Campaign in Burma *read:*

Last Ditch. They came west on a wave of military glory, to win an empire and inherit the earth. For a few months they were masters of this dream; then things went wrong. As they retreated, beset by a phoenix enemy, they found themselves in the swamps of Western Burma, hungry, hunted, and without hope. And here, 3,000 miles from home, they died. It was to have been very different.

Was it very different for anyone who was killed? Is there more point to deaths in a victorious army than a defeated army?

I did not know very well. I had never once contemplated the loss of anyone for whom I felt a shred of affection. John came level with me again.

"Was he dead?"

"Yes."

"Which Holden was it?"

"Hawk."

"Hawk!"

It hadn't looked like Hawk but I had not looked for Hawk. I had looked for someone whom I did not like or did not even know well and I had not recognised him and I had been reassured. Nobody had ever thought of Hawk's death. . . . Five years he had been in the army, training for everything . . . and now, within half an hour of the opening of the first occasion of the kind for which they had made all this effort Hawk was dead. If the selection board had stood him against a wall and shot him his death could not have appeared more pointless.
(Stephen Bagnall, 5th East Lancs Regiment, near Caen, France, June 1944)

EPITAPH FOR A FRIEND

He didn't know what fear was, some idiot wrote in some newspaper. The fool, the bloody fool, that writer. Of course he knew what fear was . . . . He knew how to overcome it, that's all. He knew how to bend fear back with the arms of will-power. . . . The struggle gets harder all the time. Will-power sweats and groans and aches and gasps for breath. . . . 'He didn't know what fear was.' Do they think they honour him by saying that? . . . Can't they see that the whole point is not that he didn't know what fear was but that he *did*?
(Captain Fred Majdalaney, 2nd Lancashire Fusiliers)

Caring for the Wounded

Medical advances ensured that the death rate among servicemen wounded in the Second World War, or suffering from disease, was much lower than in previous wars. The development of penicillin and other drugs on a mass scale, made possible by America's entry into the war, helped cure septic wounds; the development of techniques of blood transfusion helped prevent death from shock; and in the Far East methods of controlling malaria made an enormous difference, enabling more soldiers to be kept "fighting fit". The diagram shows the normal procedure for evacuating wounded men from the front line, and the help available along the way.

STRETCHER BEARERS IN THE RAILWAY CORRIDOR, BURMA, SEPTEMBER 1944

During those watery months the qualities of these men were tested to the height of endurance and they were not found lacking. Consider for a moment exactly what the men had to do. An army stretcher weighs about 30 pounds, the wounded man with his equipment will probably weigh at least 200 pounds, probably more, the bearer himself carries the same equipment as that of the infantry and, so far as jungle warfare is concerned, he must carry a weapon as well. Visualise then the load, the country, the climate, the mud, to say nothing of the attention of snipers and the prevalence of ambushes, and consider the guts and fortitude required to get the wounded in.

Under normal conditions four men carry a stretcher; the conditions under which we were then operating demanded six, four to carry and two to act as reliefs. I once watched a squad carrying a casualty through paddy fields, the bearers up to their knees in thick mud and the two spare men assisting them to extricate their legs in order that they might move at all. This particular squad had taken over five hours to cover less than three and a half miles.

(Geoffrey Foster, Chief Doctor, 36th Division)

AN ADVANCED DRESSING STATION, NORMANDY, 'D'-DAY + A FEW

I am getting overburdened again — I haven't enough stretchers for all these fellows who come in on doors and gates on the carriers. I'm out of blankets — it's getting dark and I'm very tired. The fellows in the echelon are helping and looking rather apathetic at their first sight of real injuries. They hesitate to lift a stretcher unless they can turn their backs on the injured. I'm sorry for them. . . . I'm holding five cases of exhaustion — what used to be called shell shock — and I've finally got them off to sleep, laid out on stretchers in the cover of the hedge. The guns are still banging away and the general noise occasionally wakes these heavily doped cases. They take a lot of quieting.

One case I'm holding is a great worry. Compound fracture of femur; he is very shocked and has lost a lot of blood. I've left him for a while but will have to give him blood. We lift him to near a dead tree. It begins to rain and we put up a gun cape as a shelter over his head, supported

Conditions in Italy were sometimes just as bad as in Burma. These stretcher bearers worked under a hail of mortar fire and in pouring rain to bring the wounded down the side of Monte Camino. It took three hours to get up the hill and more than three hours to bring the wounded down.

Study the expressions on the men's faces. What do they suggest to you the men are feeling? ▷

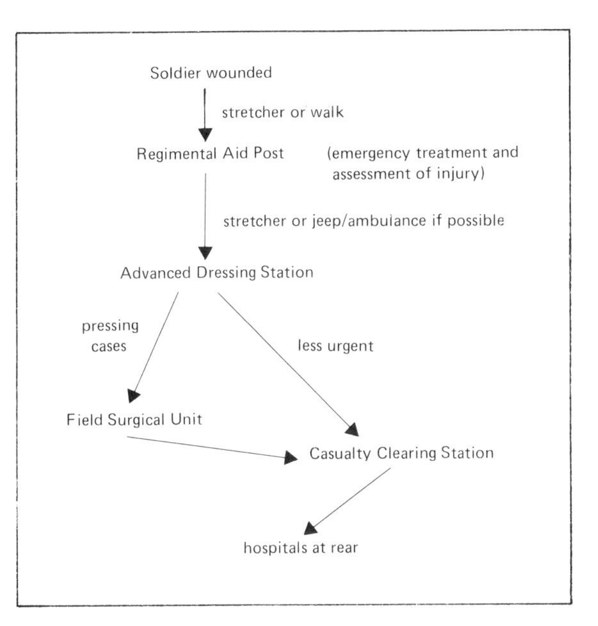

by two jerricans. I give him a blood transfusion. It all looks very off in the dark; even in the yellow light of a dimmed torch he looks grey and near to death. The first pint goes as fast as I can run it and I attach a second. He is improving already . . .

Hangers on are surprised at this surgery in the field, in the dark and rain. Fortunately his vein was fairly easy to find. Must find some better way of using a light.

(Captain D.G. Aitken, R.A.M.C., 8th Armoured Brigade)

THE BENEFITS OF PENICILLIN

The first man I tried it on was a young New Zealand officer called Newton. He had been in bed for six months with compound fractures in both legs. His sheets were saturated with pus and the heat in Cairo made the smell intolerable. He was little more than skin and bone and was running a high temperature. Normally he would have died in a very short while, as did all our wounded when infection was prolonged.

We introduced small rubber tubes into the sinuses of the left leg and injected with a very weak solution of penicillin . . . because we had so little. I gave three injections a day . . .

Out there in Cairo, I knew nothing of what was being done in England, and the thing seemed like a miracle. In ten days the left leg was cured, and in a month's time the young fellow was back on his feet.

(Lieutenant-Colonel Pulvertaft, Cairo, 1943)

Prisoners of War – Germany

Escapes from Prisoner of War Camps in Germany have been one of the most popular sources for films and stories of the Second World War. But, for the vast majority of prisoners, escape was not a possibility and they had to learn to live in conditions of considerable hardship and cope with the psychological problems which lengthy imprisonment produces for anyone.

Allied Prisoners of War carrying the daily rations at Stalag VIIA, a cosmopolitan, overcrowded and dirty camp in Bavaria. This pot contained the daily ration for 360 POWs.

EVERYDAY LIFE

New P.O.W.'s were constantly being thrust amongst us, with their torn battle-dress . . . . We no longer listened to the stories for more than the minimum time necessary . . . . We stifled our yawns, directed the conversation, as soon as it was tactful to do so, to the price of beer in the English messes, what the food was like in England, and generally to things that mattered. We would leave them talking excitedly, and would get about the really important business of the day. Who was going to draw the hot water for the tea? And why had only fourteen slices of bread been cut from that chunk? Surely anybody but a moron would have got sixteen?
(Flight Lieutenant Oliver Philpot, Stalag Luft III, Sagan, Silesia)

Rations

Rations in the Stalag were: Five potatoes a day, a little soup, 25 grammes of margarine, 50 grammes of sugar, a little jam and a piece of cheese.
(Bombardier Robert Greensmith, quoted in the *Glossop Chronicle*, 27 April 1945)

Letters from Home

Food was No. One object of existence in camp, mail from home No. Two. Some men made charts and graphs of the frequency of the mail deliveries — others had elaborate filing systems. No stock-market was ever watched more closely, or had its form and tendencies more carefully studied. The mail from England could take two months, or more — it could take ten days — it was "all according". Chunks were often cut out of letters by the German censors so that the contents read like a faulty telegram — but that alone gave the men something to do — guessing the missing words.
(Oliver Philpot)

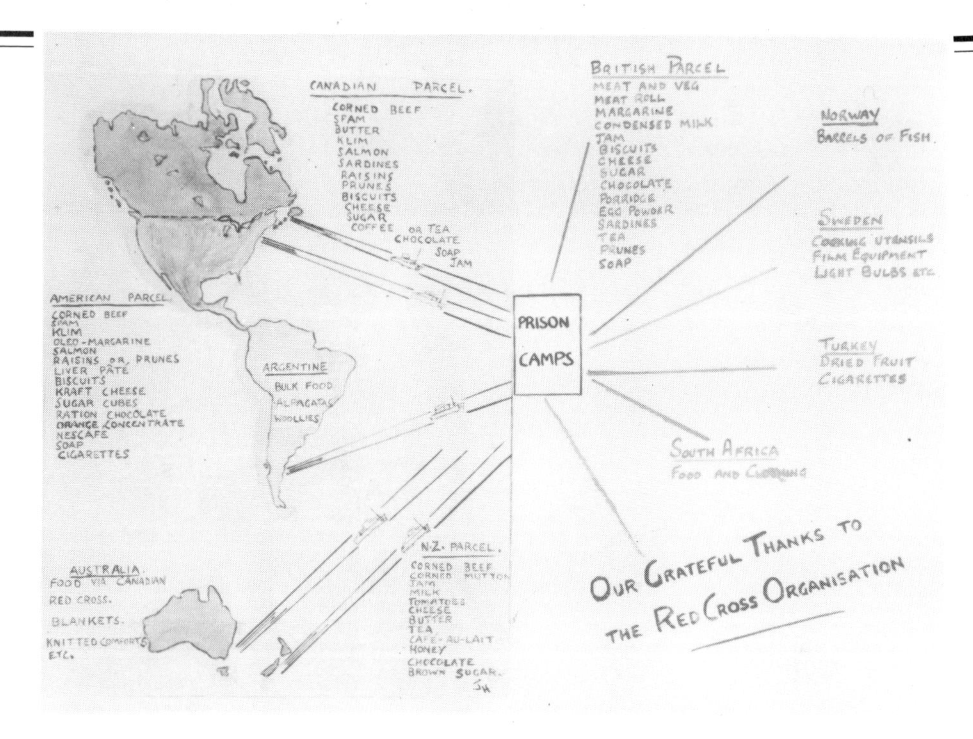

A World War Two Christmas card giving details of the contents of Red Cross parcels.

KEEPING BUSY

Under the Geneva Convention (the code governing the treatment of Prisoners of War) officers could not be set to work, but other ranks could, provided that they were paid for doing it. Many officers filled their time by studying for examinations organized by the Red Cross, the organization responsible for overseeing the care of POWs.

Exam Results

W/O Alan Saxton, who obtained first place in the Intermediate Examination of the Auctioneers' and Estate Agents' Institute last year, has repeated this success in the Final, passing with First Class Honours and being placed first in order of merit of all candidates both at home and in prisoner-of-war camps . . .

During the last month over 300 examination results have been announced the proportion of total successes being 78%.

(From *The Prisoner of War*, May 1945, official Red Cross POW newspaper)

Working in a Coal Mine

The prisoners were set to heavy work in a coal mine. They were called at 4 o'clock each morning to start work at five. And they had to work until 4 in the afternoon. The civilian workers seemed to have just as hard a time as the prisoners. Half starved they stuck grimly to their jobs. "We were made to work seven days a week," said Gunner Kenny. "Christmas Day was a holiday, but we were made to work an extra hour daily for some time afterwards to make up for it. In payment we received 26 marks a month. There was little we could spend it on."

(From an interview with returned POW, Gunner James Kenny, from a Stalag near Leipzig, in the *Glossop Chronicle*, 17 April 1945)

Do you think boredom or exhaustion would be the more difficult to cope with?

Prisoners of War – The Far East

The appalling conditions suffered by Allied prisoners and internees in Japanese Prisoner of War camps during the Second World War have been vividly described. It is important for the historian to remember two things, however. The Japanese military code of honour thought of surrender as a dreadful disgrace; and so regarded prisoners as being without honour. The Government of Japan during the war preached the racial superiority of the Japanese over other peoples and particularly taught hatred of Europeans, whom they saw as having exploited the Asian world through colonization. These points do not *excuse* the treatment many prisoners received, but they help to explain it.

RULES TO BE OBSERVED

Conditions between camps varied. Here are some rules from a camp in Hong Kong, which was described by one of its prisoners as "not too bad".

INTERNAL REGULATIONS OF THE CAPTIVES

ARTICLE 1. Although you were captured by the Dai Nippon Teikoku Army, each of you and your honour of a soldier of your native country will be recognised . . .

ARTICLE 4. Work according to the Rules of the Camp. If you disregard these rules you will be punished according to the Dai Nippon Teikoku Military Penal Codes and the Disciplinary Law . . .

ARTICLE 15. Each night from the time of Lights Out to the time of rising, under the direction of the Officer of the Day, in each of the rooms a Captive shall stand as a night guard over the sleeping men. Each will stand for an hour until relief comes to take his place . . .

ARTICLE 50 A seal of approval shall be posted on all personal books . . .

ARTICLE 60. On the way and on returning back from the fields, Captives are forbidden to leave the Group or Sing aloud under any circumstances unless have a special permission from head of the guards.

What do you think was the purpose behind Articles 15, 50, and 60?

BEHIND THE STATISTICS

Official statistics can often be brought alive by personal information. Contrast these two newspaper reports:

TERRIBLE POW DEATH ROLL IN THAILAND

It is estimated that deaths of Allied Prisoners-of-war in Thailand during the enemy occupation totalled 13,000, most of whom had been sent from Singapore. (The *Straits Times*, Saturday, 8 September, 1945)

DIED IN JAP CAMP

News has been received from the War Office that Signalman H. Mason . . . died from bronchitis at Thai Camp, Thailand on July 8th 1943. It was in 1943 that Mr. and Mrs. Mason had their first news from their son after he was reported missing at Singapore. He wrote stating that he was safe and a prisoner-of-war in Japanese hands, that he was in perfect health and they must not worry. (The *Glossop Chronicle*, 8 June 1945)

Prisoners of War after their release from a Japanese camp at Singapore. (From the collection of Max Holley.)

Leaflet dropped to Prisoner of War camps behind Japanese lines after the Japanese surrender, August 1945.

If you had been a prisoner since the fall of Singapore (February 1942), what would have been your feelings on reading this leaflet?

IN accordance with the terms of the surrender of all Japanese forces signed by His Majesty the Emperor the war has now come to an end.

These leaflets contain our instructions to Allied prisoners of war and internees whom we have told to remain quiet where they are.

Japanese guards are to ensure that the prisoners get these leaflets and that they are treated with every care and attention. Guards should then withdraw to their own quarters.

TO ALL ALLIED PRISONERS OF WAR

THE JAPANESE FORCES HAVE SURRENDERED UNCONDITIONALLY AND THE WAR IS OVER

WE will get supplies to you as soon as is humanly possible and will make arrangements to get you out but, owing to the distances involved, it may be some time before we can achieve this.

YOU will help us and yourselves if you act as follows :—

(1) Stay in your camp until you get further orders from us.

(2) Start preparing nominal rolls of personnel, giving fullest particulars.

(3) List your most urgent necessities.

(4) If you have been starved or underfed for long periods DO NOT eat large quantities of solid food, fruit or vegetables at first. It is dangerous for you to do so. Small quantities at frequent intervals are much safer and will strengthen you far more quickly. For those who are really ill or very weak, fluids such as broth and soup, making use of the water in which rice and other foods have been boiled, are much the best. Gifts of food from the local population should be cooked. We want to get you back home quickly, safe and sound, and we do not want to risk your chances from diarrhoea, dysentry and cholera at this last stage.

(5) Local authorities and/or Allied officers will take charge of your affairs in a very short time. Be guided by their advice.

The War of Propaganda

Propaganda is a method of presenting information in such a way that it produces the effect you want. It was an important indirect weapon during the Second World War, though it is difficult to assess how effective it was. Films, posters, the written word were all used in the struggle to win people's hearts and minds. The targets could be soldiers at the front, civilians at home, friends or enemies, the governments of neutral countries. Some propaganda was designed to boost morale, some to undermine it.

A British propaganda leaflet, dropped over Germany in 1940.

Was bedeutet Roosevelts Sieg?

Am 5. November 1940 wurde Franklin Delano Roosevelt zum Präsidenten der Vereinigten Staaten von Amerika gewählt.

Wer ist dieser Mann, dem als erstem in der amerikanischen Geschichte die Ehre zuteil wurde, dreimal hintereinander zu dem höchsten Amt in der freiesten Republik der Welt berufen zu werden?

Roosevelt hat in zahlreichen Reden die Diktatoren angeprangert, ihre wahren Ziele enthüllt und ihre Methoden gegeisselt.

Roosevelt hat es bewirkt, dass von Anbeginn des Krieges — und in noch viel stärkerem Masse seit dem Zusammenbruch Frankreichs — die Hilfsquellen Amerikas für die Sache Grossbritanniens eingesetzt wurden.

Roosevelt hat in seinem Entschluss, die Diktatoren zu bekämpfen, das ganze amerikanische Volk hinter sich. Während des Wahlkampfes erhob der republikanische Kandidat Wendell Willkie nur einen Vorwurf gegen diese Aussenpolitik seines Gegners Roosevelt: dass Grossbritannien noch nicht genug Hilfe bekomme. Nach der Wahl versprach Willkie seine vorbehaltlose Unterstützung aller Massnahmen zur Vermehrung der Hilfe für Grossbritannien. Jetzt erhält Grossbritannien die Hälfte der gesamten amerikanischen Kriegsproduktion.

Die Wiederwahl des Präsidenten Roosevelt bedeutet:

130 Millionen in USA sind einig gegen Hitler!

In translation:
What does Roosevelt's Victory Mean?
On 5 November 1940 Franklin Delano Roosevelt was elected President of the United States of America.

Who is this man, who, for the first time in American history, has had the honour of being called three times in succession to the highest office in the freest republic in the world?

In countless speeches Roosevelt has pilloried the dictators, revealed their true aims and castigated their methods.

Roosevelt has been responsible for the fact that from the beginning of the war – and to an even greater extent since the fall of France – American resources have been used to aid the cause of Great Britain.

In his decision to fight the dictators, Roosevelt has the whole of the American people behind him. During the election campaign the Republican Candidate Wendell Willkie raised only one objection to the foreign policy of his rival, Roosevelt: (namely) that Great Britain was not yet getting enough help. After the elections Willkie promised his whole-hearted support for all measures aimed at increasing help to Great Britain. Now Great Britain is receiving half the entire American war-output.

The re-election of President Roosevelt means that 130 millions in the USA are united against Hitler!

The map is entitled:
THE YOUNG NATIONS WITH US.
The ships contain: *airmen and soldiers*
petroleum
coffee
rubber
cotton
tin
copper
beef
mutton
wheat
tanks
guns and bombs
firearms
aeroplanes
citrus & other tropical fruits

A German propaganda leaflet dropped to Allied troops fighting in Italy, winter/spring 1944/45. ▷

ONE MORE RIVER!

But it isn't only "one more river" - this time it is THE river!

It is the mighty Po!

Do you remember the hell of the rivers Sangro, Rapido, Liri, Volturno and Garigliano? Do you remember the lives that were sacrificed in crossing these rivers?

Put these rivers all together and the result will be smaller than the

Po!

Also when you crossed these rivers, the Germans, were in retreat and had no time to prepare defenses.

But covering the Po you will find a blanket of death... Artillery, Nebelwerfers, Mortars and Spandaus.

The whole Po area is a network of canals and is impassable for tanks.

Rush
In!
Various
Exiting
Revelations
Prepared -
Oh Boy!

And here are a few facts about the Po:

At its shallowest part (between Adda and Mincio) it is 7 ft. deep.
At the deepest part (near Pavia) it is 20 ft. deep.
The width varies from 208 to 1,040 yds.
The banks are mostly sheer and between 18 and 30 ft. high.
The speed of the Po exceeds 20 m. p. h.

"PO" means death and suffering -

P.O.W. means security and comfort!

Think it over, only

Fools rush in...!

What is each piece of propaganda trying to do and how does it try to produce its effect? Which do you think is the most successful and why?

This is a Soviet war poster, published in 1941, which would have been displayed in the streets. It says: "Napoleon was smashed — the same fate is in store for the arrogant Hitler!"

Coming Home

Through the first days of May 1945, German units surrendered to the victorious Allies. 8 May was declared Victory in Europe Day and duly celebrated by the victors. In the Far East the Japanese Government surrendered on 14 August 1945, but large areas of South East Asia still lay in Japanese hands. It was not until 12 September 1945 that the Japanese forces occupying Singapore signed the formal surrender documents.

The process of releasing men and women from the armed services began on Monday, 21 May 1945. Most people were given a Class A release, which meant that they were released into the reserve and could be called up again if necessary. Release was supposed to occur in priority of age and length of war service, but there were often delays as replacements were waited for or bureaucracy got tangled up.

A REFERENCE FOR A SOLDIER

In the Soldier's Release Book there was a space for a written testimonial:

A reliable trustworthy man of intelligence Tpr. Bush has performed his duties conscientiously, often under difficult and dangerous conditions. His moral character and general bearing have been excellent. A careful vehicle driver and has shown precision in tracings and clerical work.
Major commanding
274 Armoured Delivery Squadron, R.A.C.
21 December 1945

DEMOBILIZATION

Glossop's first Serviceman to be demobilised is home. He is L.A/C Fred Dewsnap . . . aged 53.
"The next day (Tuesday) we were demobilised. Everything went like clockwork. I started at 8.45 a.m. and was finished and waiting for a train home at 11 a.m. The various stores we went in had the appearance of Selfridge's. Men were there to measure you and no misfits were handed out. A variety of cloths were on view to choose from and when I walked out I had a complete set of clothing."
(*Glossop Chronicle*, 22 May 1945)

Leaving the Navy

We joined a Russian ship at Malta bringing people back. We went to Toulon and slept in a great big park — and everybody was coming home and that was the route to come home by. There we were in this darn big park and as people got out of their beds to get on the train to go home so others got into their beds, waiting for the next train. They'd scooped out the earth and there was canvas and that was it. You weren't allowed out of the park. We went to Dieppe and crossed the channel into Portsmouth; into a big shed; given a trilby hat, a pair of trousers, a mac and a pair of shoes and that was it. You can imagine what we looked like. They said if it went on your head it fit. And we got a gratuity — £90 — that was your payment really for all the effort you'd done in the war. That was February 26th 1946.
(Peter Davies, recalled in 1983)

". . . no misfits were handed out"; " . . . if it went on your head it fit". Can both Peter Davies and Fred Dewsnap be right? How do you account for the differences in their experiences?

Provisional Interim Trade Certificate

During his service in the Royal Navy Max Holley

has been employed on duties appertaining to the Trade of

Sick Berth with the various aspects of which he

has shown himself fully conversant, either through his prior experience

in the Trade, or by training in the work, and employment thereon,

which he has had since his entry into the Navy.

His substantive rating on discharge was

His non-substantive rating on discharge was

Enquiries regarding this man's character and efficiency during

his period of service in the Royal Navy should be made to the

Commodore, R.N. Barracks, Devonport.

for Commodore.

R.N. Barracks, Devonport.

23rd September 194

684 Admy. 6-46 5m

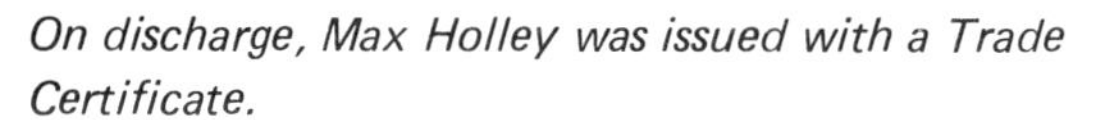

On discharge, Max Holley was issued with a Trade Certificate.

Services of thanksgiving were held throughout Britain and wherever Allied forces were serving overseas. This is the programme for a service held on 13 May 1945 (after VE Day) at a convalescent depot for the sick and wounded in Riccione, Italy.

What do you think the clothes, the pay, the certificate or testimonial were intended to help with?

WELCOME HOME

FIRST SINGAPORE MEN HOME
A REAL "WELCOME HOME" ON NORFOLK SQUARE

A telephone message on Friday morning saying that an unnamed soldier would arrive at three o'clock resulted in the Mayor and Mayoress — and many of the population of Glossop — giving the lads a home coming of which the town can be proud . . .

Following the telephone call from Liverpool on Friday morning preparations were made for a civic welcome. The POW was expected by three o'clock and at that time a large crowd assembled and loud-speaker music was playing. Half-an-hour later a 'bus arrived and was immediately surrounded by a surging mass. It was David Orme. To the strains of "There'll Always be An England", cigarettes were thrust into his hands and he was carried forward to be welcomed by the Mayor and Mayoress.

"There is no need to tell you with what sincerity and gladness I welcome David Orme back to his native town," said the Mayor.

"Thank God he has returned!"

Overwhelmed by his reception, David said he was glad to be home and then made his way up to Whitfield.

(*Glossop Chronicle*, 19 October 1945)

Date List

1939	1 September	Germany invades Poland
	2 September	Military Service introduced in Britain
	3 September	Britain and France declare war on Germany
1940	9 April	Germany invades Denmark and Norway Denmark surrenders
	10 May	Germany invades Holland and Belgium Churchill becomes Prime Minister in Britain
	27 May-4 June	BEF evacuated
	10 June	Italy declares war on Britain and France
	22 June	France surrenders
	10 July-September	The Battle of Britain
	7 September	Daylight bombing of London
	about 5 October	End of German daylight bombing
1941	6 April	Germany invades Yugoslavia and Greece
	1 June	British evacuate Crete
	22 June	Germany invades USSR
	18 November	British 8th Army offensive in Libya — "Crusader"
	7 December	Pearl Harbour
	8 December	Japanese land in Malaya
	10 December	HMS *Repulse* and *Prince of Wales* sunk by Japanese
	14 December	German retreat from Moscow
1942	15 January	Japanese invade Burma
	15 February	Singapore surrenders
	8 May	Myitkyina occupied
	20 May	All Burma in Japanese hands
	6 September	Germans halted at Stalingrad
	23 October-4 November	Battle of El Alamein
1943	23 January	8th Army enters Tripoli
	31 January	German surrender at Stalingrad
	6 February	Japanese evacuate Guadalcanal
	7 May	Tunis and Bizerta in Allied hands
	16/17 May	Dam Busters raid
	10 July	Allies invade Sicily
	3 August	Soviet offensive begins
	3 September	Allies invade Italy
	November-March 1944	Regular RAF raids on Berlin
1944	6 June	Allied landings in Normandy
	12/13 June	First V1 raids on Britain
	9 July	British take Caen
	3 August	British retake Myitkyina
	25 August	Allies enter Paris
	8 September	First V2 raids on Britain
1945	20 March	British enter Mandalay
	27 March	Last V2 raid
	2 May	Surrender of German units in Italy
	8 May	Victory in Europe Day
	6 August	Atomic bomb dropped on Hiroshima
	9 August	Atomic bomb dropped on Nagasaki
	14 August	Japanese surrender
	5 September	Singapore reoccupied by Allies

Difficult Words

ablutions wash house
ace a particularly successful individual service-man
ack-ack anti-aircraft
airbursts shells exploding in the air, not on impact
amphibious a land vehicle capable of going through water; an amphibious attack was one mounted from the sea onto land
angels friendly aircraft (the number following refers to height at which the aircraft were to fly)
armour usually refers to tanks but can also mean armoured cars
artillery large guns
balloon cables the cables attached to anti-aircraft balloons, designed to catch low-flying aircraft
bandits enemy aircraft
blitz blanket bombing
bridge the control centre of a ship, where the captain directs operations
Bully Beef corned beef
cookies RAF slang for bombs
Dai Nippon Teikoku Japanese Imperial Army
'D'-Day usually refers to the Allied invasion of Normandy (6 June 1944), but can refer to the launching of any attack
doodle German V1 flying bombs
duration, the the length of the war
echelon troops supplying the front line
femur the thigh bone
flak anti-aircraft fire
4-inch guns (HMS *Foylebank*) Mk.XVI, breech loading 45 calibre. Crew of 9. Range 18,000 yards. Rate of fire 20 rounds/minute
Ghurkas members of the British Army recruited in Nepal
hurdy-gurdy a barrel organ
infantry foot soldiers
jerrican a 2-gallon can for petrol
Junker German dive-bomber aircraft
Labour Exchange used during the war as the centre where civilians reported to register for call-up
Limpopo River, great grey, green greasy a reference from Kipling's *Just So Stories,* "The Elephant's Child".
Luftwaffe German Airforce
mess eating and relaxation area for troops
Messerschmidt German fighter aircraft
multiple pom-pom (HMS *Foylebank*) Vickers M Mk VII. Crew of seven. Range 3,800 yards. Four barrels. Rate of fire 98 rounds/barrel/minute
muster to enrol in a branch of the service
nissen hut temporary hut, usually semi-circular in shape and often made of corrugated sheeting
Panzer German tank
PIAT mortar anti-tank hand gun
posted sent to new duties
Quakers a religious group, founded in the seventeenth century, who oppose wars and violence
Samurai ancient Japanese warrior class, with a code of honour comparable with that of mediaeval knights
scramble take off in aircraft at once
sortie from the French for "exit" – going out on a mission
stalag camp
Stuka a common name for the Junkers 88 German dive-bomber
swastika broken cross emblem of the Nazi Party

You should be able to find the meaning of any other difficult words in a dictionary

Abbreviations

A.C.W.	aircraft woman
A.T.S.	Auxiliary Territorial Service
C-in-C	Commander in Chief
d	old penny
Div	division
Do.215	Dornier 215, German aircraft
e/a	enemy aircraft
E.N.S.A.	Entertainments National Service Association
F.O.	Flying Officer
G.O.C-in-C	General Officer Commander in Chief
Gnr	Gunner
H.Q.	Head Quarters
H.M.H.S.	His Majesty's Hospital Ship
H.M.S.	His Majesty's Ship
Ju 88	Junkers 88
L.A/C	Leading Aircraft man
Me	Messerschmidt (German aircraft)
N.F.T.	Night Flying Training
N.C.O.	Non-Commissioned Officer
P.O.	Pilot Officer
P.O.W.	Prisoner of War
R.S.M.	Regimental Sergeant Major
R.A.F.	Royal Air Force
R.A.C.	Royal Armoured Corps
R.A.M.C.	Royal Army Medical Corps
R.N.	Royal Navy
R.T.R.	Royal Tank Regiment
Rs	rupees (Indian currency)
s	shilling
S.B.A.(D)	Sick Berth Attendant (Dental)
S.E.A.C.	South East Asia Command
S.S.	Steam Ship
Tpr	Trooper
U.S.A.A.F.	United States of America Air Force
V.E.	Victory in Europe
W/O	Warrant Officer
W.A.A.F.	Women's Auxiliary Air Force

The Main Participants in the War

COUNTRY	DATE OF ENTRY INTO WAR
THE ALLIES	
The United Kingdom and Empire	3 September 1939
France	3 September 1939
The Soviet Union	22 June 1941
The United States	7 December 1941
THE AXIS	
Germany	3 September 1939
Italy	10 July 1940
Japan	7 December 1941

Acknowledgments, continued from page 2.

Page 9 "We hit the earth", page 11 "I would rather" and page 32-33 "Round a bend" from S. Bagnall, *The Attack*, 1947
Page 9 "An observer" from G. Wilson, *Brave Company*, 1951
Page 9 "At night" from *War Report*, ed. D. Hawkins, O.U.P., 1946
Page 10 "It was late" and "On 21st October" and page 24 "As the summer" from *Tanks Across the Desert, the War Diary of Jake Wardrop*, ed. George Forty, William Kimber, 1981
Page 11 "Five men" from Erskine, *The Scots Guards 1919-1945*, William Clowes, 1956
Page 16 "The intensity", page 17 "Perhaps it was" and "Hardly a" and page 32 "Now I had" from Geoffrey Page, *Tale of a Guinea Pig*, Pelham Books, 1981
Pages 16 and 18 Log book extracts, page 21 A. Laws diary, page 23 Letter, page 29 "Compo rations", page 34-35 "I am getting", page 38 "Internal Regulations", IWM Archives
Page 18 "Like a fleet" and page 19 "As we flew" from Gibson, *Enemy Coast Ahead*, Michael Jackson, 1946
Page 22 "My time" and page 23 "Oliver was" from *A Cackhanded War*, first published by Thames and Hudson Ltd, and reissued by Hamish Hamilton Ltd, © Edward Blishen 1972
Page 26 "It is thickly" (Yates), page 27 "Pinbaw" and page 34 "During those" from Geoffrey Foster, *36th Division, The Campaign in North Burma*
Page 28 "Supply dropping" from *The Burma Campaign*, 1946, by permission of the Controller of H.M.S.O.
Page 33 "He didn't know" from Fred Majdalaney, *Cassino*, by permission of the estate of the late Fred Majdalaney
Page 35 Pulvertaft, quoted in *The Life of Alexander Fleming*, Penguin, 1971
Page 36 "New POWs" and "Letters from home" from Oliver Philpot, *Stolen Journey*, 1950

EUROPE IN THE SECOND WORLD WAR (1942)
KEY
Neutral countries
Germany and her allies "Axis"
German occupied countries
United Kingdom
Countries occupied by U.K.
0
400
800
Km
Reykjavik
ICELAND
Narvik
Archangel
NORWAY
SWEDEN
FINLAND
BALTIC SEA
Leningrad
ESTONIA
LATVIA
LITHUANIA
E. PRUSSIA
Moscow
U.S.S.R.
Scapa Flow
NORTH SEA
Glasgow
Londonderry
UNITED KINGDOM
EIRE
Liverpool
Coventry
Bristol
London
DENMARK
Kiel Canal
Berlin
Danzig
NETHERLANDS
Dunkirk
BELGIUM
Torgau
Dresden
Warsaw
POLAND
Caen
Paris
Cologne
LUXEMBOURG
Kiev
Stalingrad
GERMANY
CZECHOSLOVAKIA
FRANCE
Vienna
SWITZERLAND
AUSTRIA
HUNGARY
CASPIAN SEA
occupied Nov.1942
ITALY
ROUMANIA
PORTUGAL
SPAIN
YUGOSLAVIA
BLACK SEA
BULGARIA
Rome
ALBANIA
Capua
GREECE
TURKEY
ATLANTIC OCEAN
MEDITERRANEAN SEA
MALTA
CRETE
CYPRUS

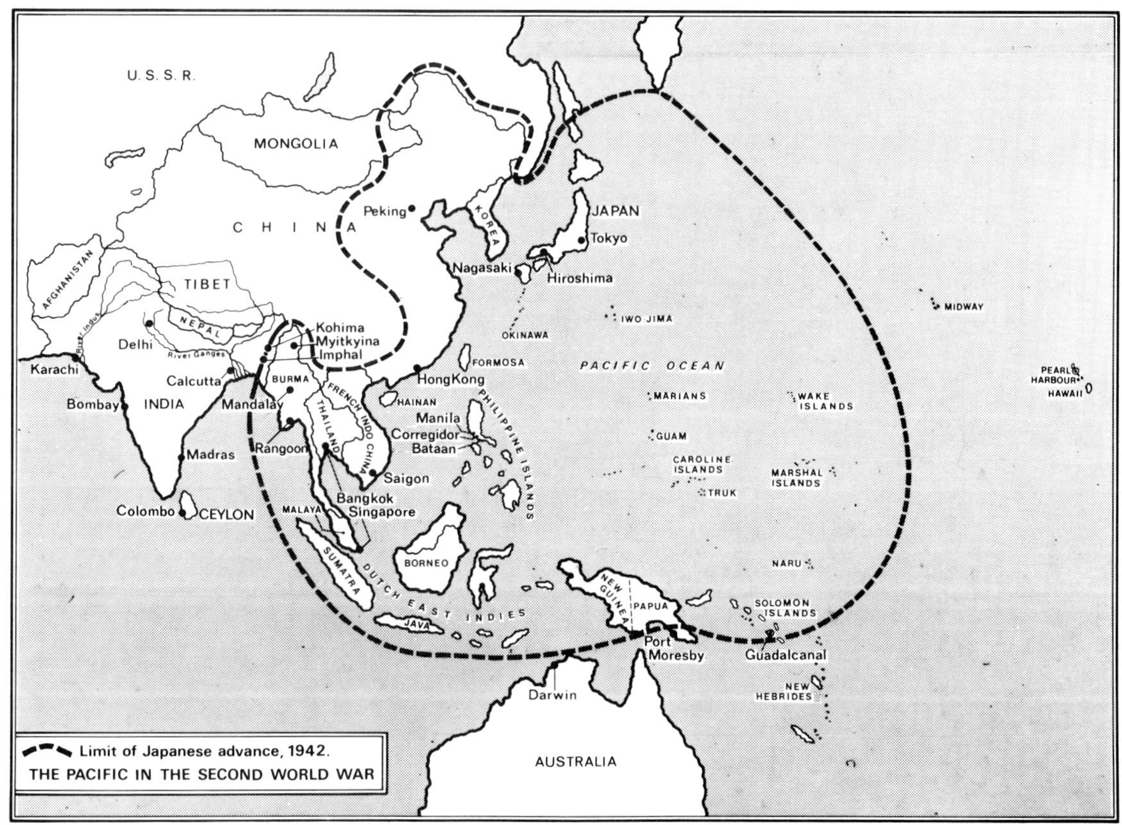
U.S.S.R.
MONGOLIA
Peking
KOREA
JAPAN
Tokyo
C H I N A
Nagasaki
Hiroshima
AFGHANISTAN
TIBET
NEPAL
River Indus
Kohima
Myitkyina
Imphal
Delhi
River Ganges
Karachi
Calcutta
HongKong
FORMOSA
OKINAWA
IWO JIMA
MIDWAY
PACIFIC OCEAN
PEARL HARBOUR
HAWAII
BURMA
FRENCH INDO CHINA
HAINAN
Bombay
INDIA
Mandalay
THAILAND
Manila
Corregidor
Bataan
PHILIPPINE ISLANDS
MARIANS
WAKE ISLANDS
GUAM
Rangoon
Madras
Saigon
CAROLINE ISLANDS
MARSHAL ISLANDS
TRUK
Colombo
CEYLON
Bangkok
Singapore
MALAYA
SUMATRA
BORNEO
DUTCH EAST INDIES
JAVA
NEW GUINEA
PAPUA
NARU
SOLOMON ISLANDS
Port Moresby
Guadalcanal
Darwin
NEW HEBRIDES
AUSTRALIA
Limit of Japanese advance, 1942.
THE PACIFIC IN THE SECOND WORLD WAR

Index